SOME PRINCIPLES OF HOROSCOPIC DELINEATION

SOME PRINCIPLES OF HOROSCOPIC DELINEATION

TOGETHER WITH CHAPTERS ON INFANT
MORTALITY AND LONGEVITY, SUICIDE
AND INSANITY, AND VIOLENT CRIME

by

CHARLES E. O. CARTER

Author of

The Encyclopaedia of Psychological Astrology
The Principles of Astrology
The Seven Great Problems of Astrology
The Zodiac and the Soul
Symbolic Directions in Modern Astrology
The Astrological Aspects
The Astrology of Accidents

BEL AIR MARYLAND
ASTROLOGY CLASSICS
207 VICTORY LANE

ISBN-10   1 933303 27 1
ISBN-13   978 1 933303 27 7

Charles Carter was born at Parkstone, Dorset,
on 31 January 1887, at 11:01 pm.

He died on 4 October, 1968, 4:30 pm, London.

Published 2009 by
Astrology Classics

The publishing division of
The Astrology Center of America
207 Victory Lane
Bel Air MD 21014

On line at AstroAmerica.com

CONTENTS

PAGE

FOREWORD 7

CHAPTER

1. THE SCOPE OF THE NATIVITY . . 11

2. THE ASPECTS 17

3. MUNDANE POSITION 29

4. SIGN-POSITION 38

5. PLANETARY PSYCHOLOGY . . . 47

6. INFANT MORTALITY AND LONG-
   EVITY 64

7. SUICIDE AND INSANITY 73

8. THE VIOLENT CRIMINAL . . . 86

9. OUTSTANDING ABILITY AND
   FAILURE 108

10. DIRECTIONAL DELINEATION . . 126

EXAMPLE HOROSCOPES

		PAGE
1.	LORD BIRKENHEAD	24
2.	IVAR KREUGER	75
3.	OCTOGENARIAN SUICIDE	78
4.	FEMALE SUICIDE	80
5.	FEMALE SUICIDE	82
6.	NURSE CAVELL	87
7.	ANGERSTEIN	100
8.	HAARMAN	102
9.	KUERTEN	104
10.	A GANGSTER	106
11.	SENATOR MARCONI	110
12.	GEORGE WASHINGTON	111
13.	BURMESE PRODIGY	114
14.	FRANKLIN D. ROOSEVELT	120

FOREWORD

MOST text-books, including the one for which I am personally responsible, are mainly of an analytical character and do not attempt to guide the reader far along the path that leads to proficiency in horoscopic delineation. In fact, few attempts have been made to attack this problem, and for a good reason—it is so difficult. Delineation is an art and it cannot be taught as one teaches merely factual knowledge. It comes with experience, if the student have the right inborn aptitudes; that is all that can be said.

However, there seems to me to be a sort of borderland that lies beyond the realms of purely text-book teaching and yet is within the scope of instruction. No one can make a student into a good delineator, and, on the other hand, almost anyone with moderate teaching ability can inculcate the alphabet of astrology: between these two extremes there is a field wherein, I think, experience can help inexperience and some general principles can be formulated and explained. This is what I have attempted here, illustrating my ideas in separate chapters that deal with important classes of psychological condition. The book is designed to follow *The Principles of Astrology* and may be read in conjunction with *The Astrological Aspects* and *The Encyclopaedia of Psychological Astrology*.

In the main I have sought to avoid in the body of

the work controversial matters that would, in that place, be unprofitable.

For example, there is much discussion nowadays as to the advisibility of abandoning the system of house-division in common use, called the semi-arc or Placidean, in favour of one of three or four others, all of which possess enthusiastic adherents. The semi-arc system is declared to be mathematically unsound. That of Campanus, or Campanella, a medieval scholar of great attainments, makes a great appeal by reason of its logical character and simplicity of conception, though it is not convenient in use because it inclines to increase the size of the houses that lie adjacent to the horizon at the expense of those that flank the meridian, causing double interception even in the latitude of London. There is also the method of Regiomontanus, a German archbishop of earlier date than that of Campanus. This system is perhaps less logical than that of the Italian, but is not very dissimilar in theory. In practice it produces maps that differ little from those erected by the semi-arc method. A third system is that of equal houses, ascribed to Ptolemy. Here the ascendant is ascertained in the usual way and each successive cusp is found by adding 30°, 60°, 90°, and so on to it. The M.C. is no longer necessarily or often the same as the cusp of the 10th and becomes a sensitive directional point. I consider this method has real value. A fourth method is that called after the Neo-Platonist Porphyry and used nowadays by the editor of *The British Journal of Astrology*. Here the angles are found in the usual way and the four quadrants of the ecliptic that are formed by them are equally trisected.

As I do not consider that an unanswerable case has,

8

as yet, been made for any particular system, I have used in this book the Placidean themes which are familiar to all.

It is, of course, not necessary to suppose that any system of house-division is correct to the exclusion of all others, though the adherents of the various modes, in their enthusiasm for the faith that is in them, always seem to assume that there can be but one correct scheme—an assumption that certainly is not self-evident.

A problem that is closely related to house-division is that which has been raised in late years about the nature of the house-cusps. For almost twenty-five years I have regarded the cusps as the boundaries of the houses, and I believe that at least ninety-nine out of every hundred astrologers have done the same. Nor do I consider that cusps have any orbs, but, as planets undoubtedly have them, a body within about 7° of a cusp will naturally shed a certain influence into the house beyond it. Whilst perfectly open to conviction, I do not think that any proofs have as yet been brought forward that this view is not correct. It is often said that it is more natural to suppose that the cusp, being the strongest part of a house, should be its centre, with areas of gradually decreasing power on each side of it. This is plausible; and I would suggest that the whole matter should be approached with an open mind and carefully investigated. I am sure that what most students would appreciate would be a demonstration of the superiority of the new point of view in judging certain well-known maps. Theoretical discussion is useful enough, but it has not always led to truth, either in astrology or other sciences.

Another controversial subject is the various parts and

points in which I have personally considerable faith, but which have been left for those to study who are interested enough to insert them in the maps that follow. Such factors are certainly not of primary importance, but they would make an excellent subject for specific treatment in a work devoted to them.

The pre-natal epoch is, of course, also a subject that stands by itself and I have not introduced it into the present book.

CHARLES E. O. CARTER

March 1934

SOME PRINCIPLES OF HOROSCOPIC DELINEATION

CHAPTER ONE

THE SCOPE OF THE NATIVITY

In the very beginning of our investigation we are confronted with certain philosophical problems. We cannot safely delineate a map unless we have a true conception of its significance and scope; and even if we are not prepared to dogmatize on these problems, we ought at least to have a working-basis for our astrology.

The nativity has been compared to a set of tools, which to some extent condition the work produced by the craftsman, who is the ego behind the chart. But it has been emphasized that a good and patient craftsman can produce valuable work with inferior instruments, whilst a lazy and inefficient workman makes little use even of good implements. Thus, it is said, we cannot, without a knowledge of the essential self behind the horoscope, say with certainty what the result ot the life's activities will be. Theosophists express it that they must know the "age of soul." This, they say, is not contained in any horoscope.

If this doctrine be fully accepted it greatly reduces the value and reliability of astrology, for the student is simply as one who judges men by examining the clothes they wear, without seeing themselves at all. He is merely one who surmises without knowing. The theory is, however, convenient for those who feel that their nativities do not flatter them; they can always say that there is a remarkable ego behind the uncomplimentary diagrams that appear to condemn them.

Few real astrologers would accept a thesis so derogatory to their art, but our authors have in the past been painfully weak in theory, and no clear teaching has been put forward in place of the foregoing.

The philosopher Simplicius who lived in the reign of Justinian (the beginning of the sixth century after Christ), explains the validity of the natus by the doctrine that the soul descends into manifestation at a time when the cosmic conditions resemble itself; just as certain types of men congregate in certain parts of a city, according to their tastes and interests, so one sort of cosmic condition attracts one kind of soul, and another draws another to it. Therefore, in a general way, we can judge the type of soul from the nativity.

Again, he says, Divine Justice brings souls to birth at times appropriate to their circumstances, that is to say, theosophically speaking, at times when their nativities would agree with their *karma*.

Simplicius thus touches on the two main fields of astrological interpretation—character and destiny. There is, according to him, a twofold action: the disposition of the soul draws it to a nativity like itself, and *karma* also attracts the soul to a map that is in agreement with the soul's deserts.

The practical difficulty at once confronts us—it is the greatest obstacle to good astrological work and persists throughout our studies—that a man's disposition and his destiny may be so different; a man may be a saint in character, but he may have a destiny appropriate, one would say, to a demon. This may be explained, philosophically, by the supposition of bad *karma* from a past when he was no saint, or it may be said that the soul voluntarily, for its own ends, chooses a difficult incarnation. But the practical difficulty still remains that we have to find a good disposition and a hard destiny (or the reverse) in one and the same map.

The first answer to this problem is that the nativity does not show *moral* goodness or badness at all. The natus is a natural figure. No pun is intended, but the fact that the same root occurs in both words is significant: Nature is that which is born, and the natus is the figure of birth. The spiritual and ideal, which is eternal and omnipresent, is above both Nature and the nativity and finds no place in them except by reflection. We may totally cut out from practical astrology all spiritual considerations, as completely as we would omit them from practical astronomy or botany. True, the wonders of the heavens and the beauties of the meadow are full of spiritual significance and may be spiritually regarded; and there *is* a similar spiritual aspect of astrology. The planets may be considered as representative of ideals; but, in so far as man is able directly to contemplate these ideals, it is not necessary to go to astrology to find them.

In the natus, however, man's spiritual character (i.e. his perception and realization of goodness, truth, and beauty) is not directly shown.

However, certain types of map are such as commonly indicate a primitive psychology in the native, probably for the reason stated by Simplicius.

This type we shall presently examine, but we may at once say that the question is by no means one of good and bad aspects, so called.

The trine and sextile are contacts of concord and they do not as a rule occur in great predominance in the nativities of vigorous, daring characters. Therefore they are not common in criminal maps, not because they indicate a "good" character, but because they tend to indicate a rather indolent one. On the other hand such "bad" aspects (i.e. oppositions, squares, and cognate contacts) as occur in a criminal map really do not so much point to the man's criminality as to his virtues, e.g. daring and courage.

Aspects of discord, or antagonistic aspects, as we may better call the opposition and its derivatives, denote a life of combat, but, in themselves, they do not point either to criminality or to right living; they are simply *non-conformative*.

A predominance of trine and sextile aspects, signifying as it does an easy-going disposition, rarely occurs in the map of a criminal, for the criminal, or at least the detected criminal (and we have few if any maps of those who were *not* detected), does not live an easy-going life. But this absence does not represent badness, but dangerous and often painful experiences. Those criminals who have a very succcessful career up to a point often have many harmonious contacts to show the more fortunate episodes in their lives. The colossal swindler, Ivar Kreuger, whose map appears on page 75, has ♀ and ♃ rising and far more technically "good" contacts than "bad" ones, ♃ being △ ☽ and ☌ ☉ ☿. If morality entered into natal astrology, his natus should have been a terrible one.

What, then, does the nativity portray?

We may say that as a rule it is a good key to that very important part of man which we may call *temperament* or *disposition*. Character is too fine a word.

We mean that part of the human psychology which is truly natural, or born with him.

Do we say, then, that the nativity shows no acquired characteristics?

Astrologically speaking, there are no such things. If, through contact with others or with special circumstances, we develop fresh traits, these will only be those shown in the natus, which have lain idle until evoked by appropriate stimuli. Man can acquire nothing; he can only unfold the potential into the actual. And his natus will show these potentialities, so far as they concern this life, and, be it always remembered, so far as they are natural. If they concern reason and the spiritual life, the nativity has nothing to say to them whatsoever.

Temperament, nevertheless, covers a vast and an important field, and it can be accurately extracted from the nativity.

Unquestionably destiny, the second great division of astrological work, can likewise be delineated—in my view with as much certainty as temperament. Spiritual activity may alter the temperament, but it seems as if, once born, the soul is bound to a certain type of destiny almost, if not quite, inexorably. I do not by this mean an absolute fatalism. I do not mean that, in an astrological sense, the hairs of our heads are numbered, but that the broad outline of our life is fairly fixed. As rational beings we shall always have a freedom of choice, but there will also be a fatal element in our lives, according to our horoscopes of birth.

In the primitive person this fatal element is everything—or almost everything. It sways his choices and his actions; he floats with the stream of stellar influence.

In the unfolded type the fatal element becomes less and less and is, as it were, pushed outwards. Such a one gains first of all control over his own interior nature and then, perhaps, over his bodily functioning, and finally over his environment. The saint, perhaps, will be so eager to make inner progress that he will neglect all else, but integral development must to call for a complete unfoldment and a gaining of power over the external as well as the internal.

But for the great majority the fatal side of the horoscope will be much in evidence and the main character and course of the external life, as well as nine-tenths of the inner life, may be accurately extracted from the nativity.

It is hoped that in this chapter a coherent and likely basis for interpretation has been established, and one, too, that squares with facts. The student must be prepared to hear of those who claim to erect maps that show the "essential self," "real ego," and so forth. But maps that are based on natural factors can necessarily only depict what is natural and only a preposterous philosophy can indulge in contrary dreams.

CHAPTER TWO

THE ASPECTS

WE have already expressed our view that the division into good and bad aspects is misleading so far as moral goodness and badness are concerned, but we may now be asked whether the distinction is still true in terms of worldly and corporeal welfare and misfortune. That is to say, can we call the trine and sextile fortunate aspects and the oppositions and squares unfortunate?

It is very doubtful if we can do so without reservations. Some astrologers of considerable experience and acumen have even gone so far as to say that there is no distinction between the two classes, save that the "bad" aspects are more powerful than the "good." This they certainly are, and we may therefore argue that in a world where nothing worth while—or very little—comes without effort, the inharmonious contacts are those which are most useful, if not actually most productive of good fortune.

It is true that many good aspects tend to bestow an easy life, but they appear to diminish the powers of endurance. I have heard one such native say that, had he not been able to lead an easy life, his health would have given way completely. The easy aspects gave an easy life and so great physical hardihood was not needed, nor was it there.

The distinction does not seem so much one of goodness and badness, or of fortune and ill-fortune, but to be one of two different types of life; one that is rough, hardy, adventurous, thick-skinned, and progressive, and another that is gentle, kindly, refined, sensitive, and somewhat lazy. The ideal life would appear to comprise something of both and to have, as its astrological picture, a horoscope with mixed types of aspect, as well as sign-positions.

The grand trine, when three or more bodies form trines in the three signs of one triplicity, is typical of the too fortunate map. It was, in ancient days, regarded as definitely evil. This view can hardly be substantiated, but it often fails to produce the positive good that one would expect, were one to take it aspect by aspect and compile from a textbook the benefits which each configuration ought to bestow. It is sometimes indolent, sometimes too dependent on others, it may be criminal, desiring to make money and find pleasure easily (Landru, the French wife-murderer).

If good aspects were actually fortunate and bad ones unfortunate, we should constantly find grand trines and "fans"[1] in the maps of great people. But we do not find them; more often we find, if not grand crosses, at least "T"[1] formations and powerful squares.

Just as a knife gets its sharpness by contact with the hone, so man seems to grow sharp and strong by contact with the rough and difficult elements in life; this the native of many harmonious contacts either will not or cannot do. Hence he remains weak, and even if he is not a worldly failure, he is likely to be a psychological one.

[1] By "fan" I mean a trine with a body or bodies in sextile to both components; by a "T" I mean an opposition with a body or bodies in square to both components.

On the other hand, the much-afflicted map may run to harshness and brutality, and with some excuse, for, as the native may himself say, "I am only dealing to others what life has dealt to me."

As too harmonious a map enervates, so too afflicted a horoscope may break under sheer stress of difficulty and hardship. Yet the latter type will at least put up a good fight.

But in considering aspects regard must necessarily be had to the congeniality or otherwise of the planets involved, in respect of their essential characters. For example, Venus and Neptune are both of so gentle and weak a nature that they are probably better in opposition or square than in trine or sextile, for the harmonious contact only carries the debility further, whilst a square imports some energy. The contrary is true of Mars and Uranus: here harmony is needed and a trine or sextile may be much better than a square or opposition. Jupiter, I have noticed, is often better in square than in trine or sextile, and collections of undesirable maps are full of cases wherein Neptune has what would be called brilliant aspects to the lights. Saturn is often highly beneficial when in opposition to the Sun, at least so far as wealth is concerned. It seems, in fact, that there is scope for a most detailed study of aspectual values, considering each, not only in a general sense, but also with regard to specific fields of action. In compiling lists of examples for my book, *The Astrological Aspects*, I was constantly struck by the apparent fact that the persons with the "bad" aspects often seemed in no way worse off than the persons who composed the list representing "good" ones. In fact, had the names been mixed up, no one who was ignorant of their maps would have been able to classify them into the correct groups merely from a knowledge of their lives and dispositions.

The Moon and Mercury constantly occur in criminal maps configurated by sextile or trine with Jupiter, whilst "bad" aspects between them and Jupiter will very rarely be found in such nativities.[1] The psychological truth at the bottom of this is probably that the harmonious aspects cause the natives to seek easy ways of making money. Not, of course, that these aspects *alone* can be considered adequate evidence of criminal propensities in even mild forms! But they give the inventive faculty which a criminal will misuse.

It is true that by direction trines and sextiles seem to be definitely helpful and squares and oppositions as definitely troublesome, but even so I have met with considerable success under bad directions, the only "evil" feature being that it came as the result of hard work.

In the same way how many people who won decorations on the battlefields of the Great War did so under harmonious directions? How could they?

But just as, on a long walk, we appreciate a rest by the wayside, so it is natural that we enjoy the harmonious directions which, from time to time, and, we think, all too seldom, allow us a little repose and, so to speak, carry on for us, making things, for once, move of their own accord without our having always to keep our shoulders to the wheel. The most heroic must be grateful for these occasional aids.

And, indeed, it may plausibly be argued that the life that is entirely conducted in the spirit of the antagonistic aspects is itself as unbalanced as the existence

[1] See page 96 herein.

which yawns through the years in the arms of its trines and sextiles.

I hope I have made my meaning clear. I do not wish, so to say, to "whitewash" the opposition and the square, but to point out the true distinction, as I understand it, between what are misleadingly called good and bad influences.

The conjunction and parallel are neutral, standing midway between the harmonious and the antagonistic formations, just as the neutral bodies, the Sun, Moon, and Mercury, stand midway between the so-called benefics and the so-called malefics.

Besides the distinction we have discussed, aspects may be considered in their individual natures, which are discoverable by referring them to the corresponding house-cusps, starting from the ascendant.

Thus the semi-sextile corresponds to the 2nd and 12th cusps and will be found to be related to events of the natures of these houses, and the quincunx or inconjunct of 150° is of a 6th and 8th house nature and is frequently connected in its action with disease and death. There are, in my opinion, minor aspects of 15° and 165°, which are also, respectively, of similar natures to the semi-sextile and quincunx.

The sextile is of a 3rd and 11th house value and operates largely through the mind, whilst the trine is of a 5th and 9th value and often shows the fiery character of the corresponding signs. Owing to its airy character (Gemini and Aquarius being of that element), the sextile is often disappointing in a material sense.

The semi-square is, of course, related to the 2nd and 11th houses and the sesquiquadrate to the 5th and 8th.

The square, by reason of its relation to the meridian, powerfully affects the circumstantial life and is of all contacts the most abrupt and energetic. The opposition is significant of relationships, owing to its link with the 7th, and literally tends to bring opposition into the life as well as separations and drawing apart.

Owing to the complexity caused by the natures of the planets themselves, the houses they occupy and the signs involved in any specific configuration, these aspectual characteristics are often lost sight of, but a knowledge of them will often explain the particular action of an aspect.

Besides the many opinions that prevail as to the natures of the different aspects, there are also divergent views as to their comparative strength. George Wilde held that all aspects—and he believed in many—were of like strength; but the general belief is that the conjunction and opposition are the strongest, the trine and square coming next, the sextile third, the semi-square and sesquiquadrate fourth, and the semi-sextile and quincunx last; that is to say, if we omit the quintile and its derivatives, commonly disregarded altogether. It seems rational to believe that the three aspects corresponding to the angles (conjunction, squares, and opposition) are the strongest, i.e. the most obvious in their action. But common sense would, I think, rather expect one to believe that the other aspects that correspond to the succedent and cadent cusps (i.e. semi-sextile, sextile, trine, and quincunx) would, as a class, be equally strong with one another, whilst the third class would comprise those that measure to the middle of houses (semi-square, sesquiquadrate, and, if we accept them, 15° and 165°).

These seem to be the three classes into which aspects should fall in point of strength, but it is not, of course, the traditional classification. In any case, aspectual strength depends so much upon such factors as the signs and houses occupied, and the nearness to exactitude of the contact, that one can only judge each on its merits. It is certain that close aspects are very powerful and wide ones the reverse.

Reason and experience both support the opinion that an applying aspect is much more important than one that is in process of separation.

When we come to consider directions we have to remember that progressed aspects are but excitations of natal configurations, and just as a spark will ignite an explosive as thoroughly as a torch, so there is often but little difference in the strength of a progressed semi-square and a progressed square, and so on. It is the radical condition which counts every time. We come now to another consideration.

The student must always seek to judge configurations synthetically as well as analytically. Isolated aspects do sometimes occur, but it will usually be found that, at least in the maps of developed persons, aspects are linked together in larger formations and must be considered as integral parts of these wider values.

The strength of a nativity, in so far as it depends on aspects at all, may be judged by the principle of *integration*, to which we must give attention if we would get beyond the analytical stage of judgment. Integration implies the welding together of the distinct elements of a map into a pattern; and absence of such integration—even if only one body be left detached—will destroy the harmonious meaning of the horoscope and indicate a relatively dumb note in the life. It commonly happens that an integrated map falls into two or three distinct patterns or groups, each indicative of a separate sphere of activity.

Integration in the natus signifies completeness in the life-expression, but unless there is *some* integration there is no power to express at all. To find a map with

CASE No. 1

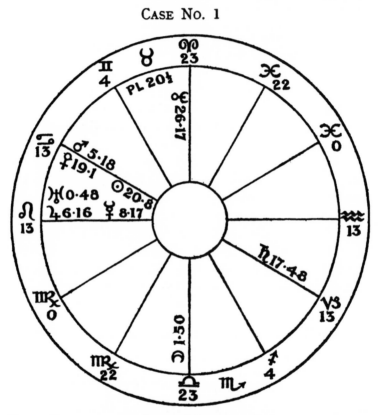

LORD BIRKENHEAD, born 6.30 a.m., July 12, 1872, at Birkenhead, Lancashire.

no aspects would be difficult, but such would be a near approach to complete non-integration.

The satellitium is the simplest form of integration,

corresponding to the conjunction and showing a concentration of force.

The grand cross and its less integrate forms, the "T" and the simple square, are examples of destructive integration.

The grand trine, "fan," and simple trine and sextile, are examples of constructive integration.

Maps that contain both elements are maps of mixed integration.

As a simple example of this principle we may refer to the natus of Lord Birkenhead, though the map of almost any characterful person would necessarily serve the same purpose.

Here the whole map falls into two formations, betraying tremendous force of character.

First, there is a conjunction of three planets—♅, ♃, and ☿. These are probably to be reckoned as being 1st-house influences and are evidential in respect of the question raised on page 9. They received the ✶ of ☽ and she, in turn, links by ☐ aspect with ♂. It is not necessary here to unravel in all its implications this marvellous group or to show how far the natural abilities and the attainments of the man are here portrayed. Five bodies are in major aspect within an orb of less than 8°.

· Second, we have ☉ ☌ ♀, ✶ PL, but ☍ ♄, all close. ♆ belongs to this group, though it is not very near. This exemplifies, by the way, what we shall say later as to the power of even inharmonious contacts between ☉ and ♄ to give wealth, though there is also in such cases the likelihood, if not the certainty, of heavy loss. In this horoscope ♄ is weak by house and aspect, though in ♑; it is also the only body on the west of the meridian. It is truly △ PL, but it would not be easy, until we know more of the latter, to say what value this contact may have had. The comparative weakness of ♄, together with the too excitable and even rude ☽ □ ♂, are the worst points in this horoscope; had ♄ been stronger, the latter would not have greatly mattered and, in any case, it probably had its uses. The native, I believe, failed when in later years he forsook law and politics for the City; and it is hardly to be questioned that a strong ♄ was what he lacked for success in finance. The first formation we have mentioned is brilliant to the last degree, but also centrifugal and excessive; and the second formation dominated by the problematic Pluto and by Neptune, could not altogether control it. It would seem that the two most powerful contacts in this map are ☿ ☌ ♃ and ☽ □ ♂,[1] and neither of these is suited for the City, though both excellent for the Bar, at which the native at one time earned £30,000 a year.

This is in the main a horoscope of personal (i.e. 1st house) self-expression; the native was a personality. And it is *expression* with which mundane position is chiefly concerned. Hence its great importance. Aspects and sign-position have this significance also, but it would be correct to say that primarily they relate to what there is to express, the nature of the ego. Mundane position renders expression easy or difficult and determines in large measure the field in which it will appear. Where, owing to inhibitive circumstances, self-expression is made difficult and consequent repressions result, it is principally the mundane positions that are to blame; the aspects may give the inherent liability to suffer distortion, but the final responsibility rests with

[1] It may be objected that ☉ ♀ ✳ PL is stronger, but ☉ and ♀ are cadent.

mundane horoscopic conditions. The extreme of non-expression is exemplified in the maps of the imbecile and mentally deficient, and it is usually found in such cases that the 3rd house is afflicted, often by the presence of a malefic on the cusp or by opposition from the cusp of the 9th. Insanity, on the other hand, which implies free distorted expression, is mainly the result of afflictive aspects and shows less in terms of the mundane scheme. However, if such a state results in incarceration, then *this* may well be indicated by a house position, e.g. important bodies in the 12th.

Actors and novelists may be taken as types who must, by virtue of their calling, have free expressive powers if they are to succeed at all.

Suicide represents a retreat or flight from life—a refusal to attempt continued manifestation in the medium offered. The principle of adjustment or self-accommodation to circumstances breaks down, but the degree of psychological responsibility must be weighed against the character of the environment which, in some cases, may be such that endurance is almost impossible. The most typical example of *deliberate* refusal to accept conditions would occur in cases like the suicide of the younger Cato, who would not remain alive under the domination of a prince.

Defective adjustment as between the ego and its environment—in which term we must really include not only the general environment but also the body and the natural part which we have called the disposition—is the source and origin of all our difficulties and is usually indicated by aspectual disharmony, which may be accentuated by sign-positions and mundane location. A good Venus makes adjustment easy; Mars makes it difficult, but gives the courage to fight to subdue what is obnoxious; Jupiter seeks hazardous solutions; Saturn wins harmony by self-abnegation or by patiently trying; Uranus is, of all planets, most impatient and Neptune most sensitive, so that both are usually prominent in suicidal maps, as we shall see in Chapter Seven.

Disease limits, and death ends, man's terrestrial self-expression and in cases of infant-mortality the term of manifestation is short and its intensity slight. Disease is a failure to establish harmony between the body and its environment, whether the cause lie in man's wrong living, as it certainly sometimes does, or in the attacks of Nature, which seems sometimes to exhibit an hostility to man. Horoscopically, disease, like suicide, is mainly a matter of aspectual tensions, playing in this case on a weak body, in that, on a weak mental condition. Certain planets tend to weaken the body by their mere mundane position and others have a contrary effect. Thus an angular Neptune always debilitates the physique to some degree and an angular Mars, though it may cause certain difficulties, always tends to harden the condition. Some mundane positions are, so far as corporeal strength goes, good; and some bad. It is probably always helpful to have planets rising and it is also likely that the simple presence of several bodies in the 6th or 12th house is unhelpful. Many bodies in negative signs are weakening; and in infant mortality this condition is one of the noticeable features.

CHAPTER THREE

MUNDANE POSITION

SINCE, in large cities, many babies are born at short intervals and within inconsiderable distances of each other, it must necessarily follow that mundane position is of immense importance, since this is the only thing that alters appreciably within a short space of time.

Mundane position includes house-position and involves the various parts and points which depend for their position on the ascending degree at any particular moment. It is usually said to affect circumstances rather than character, but it is necessary to interpret this ruling very liberally.

Very few cases are available of children born at approximately the same times and places, with particulars of their dispositions and careers, but this field would be a very rich area for astrological research. It is known that, though twins are often similar in fortunes and characters, in some cases there are very wide divergencies on both scores, and the true astrological indications of these differences or similarities, as the case may be, ought to be determinable. Some astrologers lay great stress upon the pre-natal epoch as the true key to such problems, but there should also be some explanation in terms of the nativity. If there is none, then the only logical course would be to discard the nativity altogether and use only epochs, for if the former fails in the case of twins there is no reason to suppose that it is reliable in any circumstances.

It is quite certain that the difficulty here adumbrated is a serious one and will become critical. There is an ever-growing interest in astrology, and this interest has been accompanied by signs of an attack on the part of those who either discredit the astrological claim, or, for some other reason, wish to prevent its acceptance. Many who desire to disprove the astrological thesis will seize upon the point we have raised and will seek for evidence in the form of simultaneous births and dissimilar lives. That is, if they can find them.

Astrology has already heard the mutterings of such a criticism and has always met them by the assertion that even a few minutes of difference in the birth-time may make a vast difference. That is to say, we have taken refuge in the doctrine of the importance of mundane positions; we have, in effect, said: Yes, children may be born in the same town and within a few minutes of one another, and still there may be great divergencies of nature and of destiny; such a result would not discredit astrology, because, though such children would have the same sign-positions and the same aspects, they would have dissimilar mundane configurations, and that is sufficient to account for great differences.

Thus we see that we are bound, by the logic of facts and by our own pretensions, to lay great stress on mundane position, and this is one of the first points—if not the first—to be observed when a map is laid before us for judgment.

It may be laid down as a general rule that *prominency is largely identical with proximity to the angles*, and planets fail in strength as they increase their elongation from these four cusps. The cadent houses represent that which is withdrawn and weak; the succedent houses represent an intermediate condition. Much the same is true of the cardinal, fixed, and common signs, as we shall see, and if a body is in a cadent house and a common sign, it is doubly weak; if it is cadent but in a cardinal sign there will be the desire to energize freely and openly, but there will be little opportunity. Aspects constitute a third important factor and may enable a cadent planet to come into the open, as it were. But cadency is always a great debility, so far as public work is concerned. If persons with many cadent bodies succeed in the world, it is usually by sheer mental power; thought is their strong point. They may invent and discover, but practical application is little to their taste.

When cadent the Sun indicates obscurity and lack of vital force, and Mars and Jupiter have a similar value so far as the physical energies are concerned. Neptune is a weakening, disintegrating, retiring influence, and if he is angular, whilst the vitalizing bodies are cadent, weakness of body is probable. Uranus and Pluto seem, upon the whole, to strengthen, but, like Mars, they may occasion accidents because of the vigorous type of nature which they bestow; they urge the native forward into perilous positions. The Moon angular makes for a delicate and sensitive constitution. Mercury affects chiefly the nervous system; Venus in an angle is preservative because she inclines to make the native careful and anxious to avoid strains and risk, and Saturn, though depressive, has also a preservative value.

The mundane positions of the planets operate simil-

31

arly in respect of their other fields of operations. For instance, the cadent Venus does not attract affection unless there are very potent aspects to assist her.

It is obvious that the applicability of the above is influenced in particular cases by the signs and aspects concerned, but, for the reasons we have given, it would seem that the mundane positions are by far the most important, and we would recommend the student to try to extract all he can from these before turning his attention to other factors. It is useless to try to simplify astrology, for the reason that it is not a simple subject nor does it deal with simple things; but we can at least try to place the essentials and first principles in the foreground.

Let us now examine some typical cases which may serve to illustrate our contentions.

One well-known horoscopic pair is that of Annie Besant and Field-Marshal Hindenburg. The former nativity is familiar to most astrologers; the soldier was born on the same day but with 23° Capricorn on the ascendant.

Now here there is a considerable similarity, inasmuch as both were fighters; both also attracted great devotion and raised great enthusiasm by their personalities. But Annie Besant was a rebel, a reformer, and progressive, and an occultist; Hindenburg is a conservative, willing to serve his country in any capacity, but always at heart loyal to the Hohenzollern family. He is not known to have any interest in the occult. He is not, as was Mrs. Besant, a brilliant orator.

Much of this difference appears plainly enough in the maps—from the mundane positions. The two ascendants —Uranus rising in Aries in one case, and Capricorn rising unoccupied in the other—explain the contrast between the statesman, with his plain love of duty as he learnt to understand it in boyhood, and the reformer, with her violent departures from early beliefs. Uranus possesses considerable oratorical powers and Mars rises in a degree of oratory, but in Hindenburg's case both planets are less prominent. He had, indeed, to break with the past, but he did so only externally; his heart remained true to his early conceptions. Why Mrs. Besant had an interest in occultism is not very easy to understand in the light of her horoscope, but something must be ascribed to two planets in the 12th and to Uranus rising with so many aspects. Uranus likes what is new, and, in her youth and middle-age, occultism was a new thing. Again, bodies in Cancer in the 4th might incline to astral sensitivity. Hindenburg had planets in the 8th, but they were in Libra, which has no instinct to pierce into the secrets of things.

In regard to their fortunes, the field-marshal obtained great honour in his own country and is now widely respected on account of his patriotism and devotion to duty; Mrs. Besant, in her day, underwent many public attacks and made many friends and many enemies; enjoyed great popular acclamation and saw it vanish.

It is clear that Hindenburg's map is better for consistent popularity, for he has not the same violent configurations in angular houses, though the bodies in Cancer fall in his 7th. This is a house of great public reputation, and, since both bodies are dignified, they defied the bad aspects they receive. Mars, ruling the 10th in this horoscope, is in detriment, but has good aspects.

In Mrs. Besant's case Saturn ruled the 10th and was weak by sign and by house, so that public honour did not attract her and was not spontaneously attracted to her. The bodies in the 7th were not strong by aspect and the Sun was weak by sign. The full force of the opposition to Uranus comes across the horizon, and destroyed much of her popularity from time to time, often as a result of her own acts, Uranus being in the 1st house.

Neither native was personally solicitous of fame, and this is indicated by the comparative weakness of Saturn in each map. Neither, in all likelihood, cared in the least for material wealth.

It appears that we can reconcile the differences of temperament in these cases without doing any violence to astrological teaching and practice, and we must not forget that, just as in each case the aspects and sign-positions are alike, so, if it were possible to invest-igate, it would unquestionably be found that there were many temperamental resemblances in the two illustrious natives.

Another well-known pair of horoscopes is that of Sainte-Beuve, the great French critic, and Benjamin Disraeli, the statesman. True, the latter was also an author and literatus, but I am not aware that Sainte-Beuve had any interest in politics—apparently he had unusually little for a Frenchman. There is thus a sharp distinction between the two men—one devoted his life primarily to politics, the other had no interest in them. How is this shown in their nativities?

Politics come under Saturn; but one may have various motives for entering upon a political career. For example, Ramsay MacDonald has Neptune in the 10th, which points plainly to an idealistic purpose dominating the whole life.

Disraeli seems to have been actuated by ambition; by

34

the desire to shine and to outdo others, to show that he could beat others at their own game. He had the Sun in Leo, whereas in the critic's map she was in Virgo; in the statesman's natus she is in square to three bodies in Scorpio, but in the critic's she is in sextile, a mental aspect and one that, being harmonious, inclines to a less turbulent life. Sainte-Beuve had all bodies save two on the western side of the horoscope, showing one whose interests tend to centre on *others*; Disraeli had all save two on the eastern side, denoting a much more personal type of life. In neither case was the 10th tenanted, except that Disraeli had Saturn 5° from the cusp of the 11th and Sainte-Beuve had the Sun about the same distance from the same cusp. In the former case Saturn was with Uranus, a combination pointing to the ambitious and, if possible, masterful life, whilst Sainte-Beuve had Mercury in the 11th, which is quite appropriate to the critic. The 11th indicates what we like to be, the 10th what we actually are, in each case from the standpoint of public work.

Another striking pair is that of Sir Richard Burton, the oriental explorer, and Dr. Joseph Wallace, founder of a dietetic and hygienic school of thought famous among food-reformers when the writer was a youth. These maps are very alike, as will be seen on reference to the data in *Notable Nativities*. There is, in both, the striking fact that only the Moon is above the earth, and she, being ruler of the 9th in the explorer's map and the 8th in that of the physician, seems to be the key-note to the difference in the careers. Each, of course, was an explorer, but in widely different senses. Burton was famous for his daring and his disguises, as well as for his perfect skill as an actor and linguist, which enabled him to penetrate into places where it was

35

instant death for a Christian to be found. He belonged to the group of brilliant men born when there was the conjunction of Uranus and Neptune in Capricorn about 1821. Apart from the immense importance of an isol-ated body in elevation, as the Moon is here, the main difference in mundane position (there being no zodiacal differences) is that Burton had four bodies in the 5th, whilst two more—Venus and Mars—were within 10° of the cusp; Wallace, on the other hand, had four bodies in the 4th, a much less enterprising house. A heavily occupied 4th house often goes with a scientific career.

It is a pity that we cannot compare character as well as career in these duplicate cases, especially when the maps are as alike as the last two. It would indeed be a bitter blow to astrological pretensions if there were not some striking likenesses. But I believe that such a study would reveal the truth of the position taken up in Chapter One, namely, that there is an ego behind the nativity which cannot be found in any astrological figure and which, when its powers have been unfolded, looms so large as to reduce what *is* horoscopically depicted to comparatively small dimen-sions. Thus, in comparing two such men as these, or in comparing Hindenburg with Annie Besant, the egoic part is so large, in relation to the temperamental, that we might see more difference than similarity. Idio-syncrasy has been absorbed into character and redeemed from the astrological field of influence. But only in perfect man could this process be entirely carried out. Among the average specimens of mankind the likeness between two people with the same nativities would be far more noticeable, but even these might still have no trouble in seeing that "I am I and you are you."

Of course, one of the things that will change appear-

ance and disposition very considerably is an alteration
in the aspects received by the ascendant.

I have myself met a lady born only half an hour
after myself, but the passage of the ascendant from the
conjunction of Uranus and almost exact square of
Saturn to the trine of the Sun and Venus had completely altered the appearance—and very much to the
lady's advantage. Probably Leo had also come on to
the midheaven and the sign occupying this position is
often perceptible in the physical appearance.

When we perceive what wide differences in temperament and physique appear even when two horoscopes
are in the main almost identical, we see that the
doctrine of the astrological die-hard, to the effect that
the nativity covers all things, is indeed untenable.
There is a soul which is, essentially, independent of the
horoscopic influences, although, in undertaking mundane activity, it submits itself to some extent to them.
But it does not receive the stellar impacts passively,
or, at any rate, need not do so. It has a life and vitality
of its own and can react to these influences; indeed,
the more it cultivates the idea of inherent power, the
more successfully can it do this. This does not discredit
astrology, but it does discredit that fatalistic error
which would make not only externals, but our very
inner selves, creatures of the stars. This might be true
if man were but a part of nature, as, in fact, he is
nowadays usually considered to be. But he lives a life
that is distinct and, in part, even separate from nature,
and he can aspire to a supra-natural life. Thus neither
his fortunes nor his soul is submerged in an ocean of
natural influences, whether astrological or of any other
order.

CHAPTER FOUR

SIGN-POSITION

In my view sign-position is the least obvious of the three main factors that compose the horoscope.

Let me put it this way. Tabulate twenty cases wherein Mars is in Leo, and as many more in which it is in the 5th house, and again, twenty wherein it is in conjunction with the Sun: I believe that it will be found that the last list will show the action of the conjunctions clearly, and in the second list also the value of the house-positions will be easily discernible; but, without an intimate knowledge of the dispositions of the natives, it will sometimes be found hard to discover the significance of the sign-positions.

It is also difficult to distinguish the difference between one planet in a sign and another body in the same sign. One can, of course, distinguish in theory between, let us say, Mercury in Leo and the Sun in Leo; it is easy to do so. But it is not so easy to discover the actual difference in disposition in two individuals respectively having these positions.

Again, try to distinguish Saturn in Cancer on the M.C. and the same planet in Capricorn in the same mundane position. Again we can talk easily enough as to what the difference *should* be, but in actual practice the distinction is not so easy, and I believe that, in such a configuration, roughly two-fifths of the totality

38

of significance is derived from the planet and as much to the mundane position, whilst only about a fifth can be ascribed to the sign concerned.

Sign-position, I venture to assert, is the finer shading of the nativity, and requires the deepest insight into character for its understanding as well as the most effective mastery of language for its expression.

Even the ascending sign, whilst very prominent in most cases, may be overshadowed by a rising planet. Supposing you had to hit off the most striking parts of a man's character, would you rather know what planet he had rising but not what sign, or what sign was on the ascendant, but not what planet? Personally I would certainly prefer that, if there were to be one or other limitation on my knowledge, I should know the rising planet, Neptune being, perhaps, the body which seems as a rule to modify the rising sign least. This, of course, by reason of its mild nature.

This statement must not be misunderstood as an affirmation of the non-importance of sign-values, but of their true relative value. I have tried to write on this subject, but I have been forced to the conclusion that, whilst one could do so from a theoretical point of view (as, in fact, others have already done), a treatise based on actual cases is impossible, inasmuch as an intimate knowledge of enough lives is unobtainable. And only a very great familiarity with temperament reveals the action of the sign-positions, at least in the majority of cases.

In this work I feel called upon to attempt some solution, or at least to express an opinion, upon the vexed and difficult problem of what we may continue, in medieval language, to call the planetary dignities.

In my *Astrological Aspects* I have expressed the view

that aspectual values may be modified by sign-position values, e.g. it is better to have a square between dignified bodies than a trine between debilitated ones.

While writing *The Astrology of Accidents* fresh knowledge forced me to reconsider this view, for it became evident, from the tables therein printed, that planets—or at least several of them—reach their maxima values as indications of accidents when in their own negative dignities. This was shown to be the case in regard to the Moon, Jupiter, and Saturn, and Mars may almost be included, though his actual maximum was reached in Virgo. Of course it is admitted that the number of cases used cannot be regarded as sufficient to prove that these *are* the actual maxima, but it does probably suffice to show that these bodies are certainly not *less* liable to cause accidents when in these signs. And, if they are not well-placed from the accident-standpoint when in their negative dignities, it seems reasonable to suppose that they would also not be helpful from any other, for accidents are but one manifestation of disharmony. Thus a physical fall is but a specialized form of a tendency of which a fall from power (socially, politically, or economically) would be another.

Note that the table in question contains no evidence that the positive dignities are good; they, in turn, seem to be of indifferent value so far as accidents are concerned and I have never seen any statistical evidence that they have any special significance at all.

In a word, the table in *Accidents* implies that the positive dignities are meaningless and the negative ones are, at least in some cases, bad.

What is necessary is further statistical research to decide, if possible, whether (a) there is anything in sign-position at all;[1] (*b*) whether there is any truth in the traditional table of dignities and debilities and, if so, whether it is applicable in a general sense or only in a special sense and, if the latter, in what; (*c*) if the traditional tables are wrong, is there another which is valuable and, if so, is it of general application, or is each sign-position good or bad from specific points of view?

One might be tempted, pending the execution of this somewhat formidable programme, to decide that the traditional table is probably worthless and that every sign-position must be judged on its own merits, in relation to specific fields of activity. But the table in *Accidents* seems to indicate that the tradition is not groundless, but misunderstood and perhaps incorrectly handed down to us.

There is, of course, a strong belief among astrologers that the tradition of dignities is both correct and important, and I held this view myself, as mentioned above. Unfortunately, whenever I have tested the validity of this particular piece of tradition by objective methods, it has proved unreliable or definitely incorrect, and I am forced to the conclusion that, like many other things, sign-positions are good or bad according to circumstances. What these may be, only prolonged investigation can determine. Some we can guess with a fair chance of being correct, e.g. we may safely believe, for several reasons, including some statistical research, that the Sun is not well-placed in Pisces so far as longevity is concerned. But we should probably

[1] One may probably regard this as proven by (*a*) first principles, (*b*) the evidence of tradition, (*c*) our actual daily experience, (*d*) certain statistical work, which needs, however, much extension.

be correct in assuming that it is a quite good position for the occupation of nursing. Yet how often our surmises are incorrect! In *Astrology* for December 1933 it was shown, as a result of the examination of 160 cases of cavalrymen, that the Sun was *least* often in Sagittarius and Virgo: the fact that Virgo is low would surprise no one, but that Sagittarius should share this distinction seems a clear reversal of all we know about the sign in connection with horses! Truly scientific astrology is as yet but a babe; we are at the beginning of things. Tradition has been a faithful beast and has carried us for many centuries, but she is unequal to modern requirements.

It is, of course, not difficult to find isolated cases to support almost any argument. For example, the map of the ex-Kaiser might be adduced as an example of the value of mutual reception. Despite an opposition of the Sun and Saturn, involving the 2nd house, he accumulated great wealth; he was, in fact, particularly successful in this respect. But, as a matter of fact, *any* configuration of these two bodies favours money-making, as can be demonstrated by the examination of the horoscopes of the rich, though an opposition may certainly cause heavy losses. A great many of our arguments about aspects, houses, and signs are due to insufficient real knowledge. For instance, I have heard a system of house-division condemned because "it puts Jupiter into my 2nd and I am not rich." Jupiter in the 2nd, even when strong, does not necessarily confer wealth (see Case No. 2, *Encyclopaedia of Psychological Astrology*, second edition). On the other hand, Saturn in the 2nd, even when weak, is compatible with riches (see Case No. 1 in the same work).

*   *   *   *   *

SIGN-POSITION

Passing from the consideration of particular planets in particular signs we must pay attention to the general distribution of bodies in the zodiac.

As it seems that aspectual groupings and the principle of Integration relate to the power or energy in the nativity, so it appears that zodiacal distribution has to do with *balance*, and on the whole a good psychological result will follow, others things being equal, if there is not too heavy a preponderance:—

1. In the early part of the zodiac at the expense of the later, or vice versa.

2. In one quadruplicity or mode at the expense of the others.

3. In one triplicity or element at the expense of the others.

4. In positive signs or in negative.

Lack of balance and even development due to any of these four may be to some extent rectified by a mundane position or even by an aspect. For example, lack of air may be assisted by a rising Mercury or lack of fire by a rising Sun or Mars.

As regards 1 above, a preponderance of bodies in the first three signs indicates in many cases what would be often styled a *primitive* ego. This does not necessarily imply criminality and in its highest expression this type is objective, practical, and effective from a worldly point of view. But there is usually some crudeness and failure to appreciate intellectual and aesthetic values. At worst there can be violent criminality; and an examination of the maps of violent criminals will dispel any doubts that the reader may have as to the importance of this particular form of unbalance. I have certainly seen the maps of criminals of this type with the last signs heavily tenanted, but they are a marked exception.

43

This rule does not appear to apply to crimes of dishonesty.

Horoscopes containing most bodies in the last three or four signs indicate an idealistic or, in undeveloped cases, a dreamy and imaginative type. It is notorious how often those with Aquarius and Pisces heavily tenanted are unpractical and wasteful of their time, possessing small executive abilities.

The former class seem to be possessed with the energy that makes them anxious, in any given circumstances, to "do something about it" and to assert themselves.

The classes Nos. 2 and 3 above hardly call for examination, for every astrologer learns the nature of the elemental and modal types from his first textbook, unless this is particularly unpsychological. The same is true of the positive and negative classes.

It may, however, be pointed out that a modal preponderance implies aspectual affliction. One cannot have most planets in cardinal signs without danger, either of a satellitium, or of several squares and oppositions, and the same is equally true, of course, of the two other modes.

Thus too much in cardinal signs usually imports not only much energy, but a taint of destructiveness; at best a reformer, at worst a violent criminal. High intelligence often goes with cardinal afflictions.

Preponderance in fixed signs tends also, unless the bodies happen to miss being in affliction, to violence, but of a very sudden character, breaking out from a normal static condition.

Preponderance in mutable signs indicates intelligence, but vacillation, nerve tension, and irritability.

Again, taking the elements, excess of fire runs to animal spirits and sometimes to lust; or, if there is repression through some aspectual or mundane influence, to hysteria, religious mania, and so forth. Air runs to daydreams, fantasy, waste of time, hair-splitting, shirking of hard work and the "if" habit. Water is superstitious, commonplace, trivial, and without vision. Earth is stupid and indolent, stubborn and rude.

Too many bodies in positive signs, which means, of course, an excess in fire and air, implies the unpractical, excitable, head-in-the-clouds individual, and excess in the negative signs makes for the commonplace and pedestrian attitude, life in a rut: "what can be better than a rut, if it be a pleasant one?" as one of this category remarked to me.

Distinct values attach to the various elemental conflicts which the natures and positions of the signs make possible.

Thus:

Fire–Air in conflict (i.e. an opposition from Aries to Libra) tends to great excitability, some vanity, and the overthrow of the mental clarity in emotional storms.

Fire–Water is even more highly excitable, but here the emotions do not affect the mind but create their own tumult and riot. A square from Aries to Cancer, for example, is a most turbulent influence, as seen in the nativity of Isadora Duncan (born 2.33 a.m., May 27, 1878, San Francisco).

This combination inclines strongly to so-called psychic tendencies and uncontrolled imagination.

Fire–Earth is much steadier and produces checks and disappointments, environmental difficulties, conditions of stasis.

Earth–Water has been said to create a figurative pool of mud; there is a sensual tendency, indolence, and a desire for comfort.

Earth–Air has a chiefly mental effect, inclining to obstinacy and narrowness, mental immobility of some kind and, at times, some inhibition of the senses, such as deafness.

Air–Water is the parent of many inordinate mental conditions, since the fantasy here impinges adversely on the mind. Phobic states arise and fears—fear of the dark, of solitude, of crowds, of open spaces, etc. There may be superstition.

Naturally these are given as hints only and must in every case be judged in relation to the bodies involved. The benefic contacts are, of course, always in the same element (trine) or the same polarity (sextile).

*   *   *   *   *

We may now restate the three leading conceptions which have here been attached to aspects, mundane positions and sign-positions, namely, power, freedom of expression or the contrary, and balance.

Like all our astrological ideas these must not be applied too rigidly, for there is a constant and wide interaction throughout the nativity; the stellar influence circulates through our horoscopes as does the blood through our bodies. However, these ideas may serve as useful avenues of approach and, in studying and practising the art of delineation, it seems that it is just such a base from which to start that we need.

Here, then, is our fundamental conception: an ego which seeks to express itself through its natural envelope and through a destiny which, Plato tells us, it beholds before its descent and freely chooses.

Both of these should be legible in the chart that we astrologers have before us.

CHAPTER FIVE

PLANETARY PSYCHOLOGY

IT would not be in accordance with the design of this work to introduce into it a discussion of so-called "occult" or "esoteric" philosophy, but at the outside of all astrological delineation we are met with the principle of duality which runs through the whole of manifestation. There is a perpetual alternation through all forms of natural expression, which, in the nativity, appears in the basic division of the elements of the map into those which are positive or outgoing, and those which are negative or indrawn.

The planets, headed by the Sun and the Moon, fall into these two classes, Mercury, Mars, Jupiter, and Uranus being positive, and Venus, Saturn, and Neptune negative. However, in a sense the planets are bi-sexual, since, in the traditional scheme, they have each a positive and negative sign for masculine and feminine expression. Nevertheless some planets are unmistakably processive and others recessive.

The signs fall into the traditional positive and negative alternations, and the same principle probably influences the domal values, although it is not customary to call the houses positive and negative and, in any case, it is a mistake to consider the houses simply as a mundane reflection of the signs. At all events the correspondence between the two factors is not close in practice. Because a certain vocation (let us say) is often indicated by many bodies in Scorpio, it does not in the least follow that there will also be a tendency for those who follow it to have many bodies in the 8th house. Nor because in cases of a certain malady Mars is always in a cardinal sign, does it follow that he will also be in an angle.

We thus perceive that the natus represents, from the standpoint of human life, an alternation of proceeding and returning pulsations, which probably affect man's instinctive and impulsive nature, his bodily states, and even his environmental conditions. One beat drives him outwards, under the influence of the Sun and other positives, to seek, achieve, discover, build, and destroy; the next draws him back to assimilate, store up, digest, and safeguard what he has won. The former is the Great Offensive against life and the world, the Great Adventure, the "golden road to Samarcand"; the other is the Great Defensive against life and the world, the Home-coming, the Harvest Festival.

The conception is simple, though fundamental; it is familiar to all who have considered the life that is around them understandingly, and it need not be laboured. Astrology shows clearly enough that, though some types are exceedingly inclined to outgoing activities and others have the reverse propensity, yet *all* horoscopes contain both, in some proportion.

The cardinal mode is, of course, the analogue of the proceeding aspect, and the fixed is the stationary, whilst the mutable mode is the intermediate whose outward activities are principally of a mental kind and are often carried on from within doors.

It is not to be thought, of course, that the negative attitude is necessarily a total failure to express and a loss of life's opportunities. Its expression is, to be some-what paradoxical, an inward motion and consists in the interior life of the soul. It may involve as much activity, or more, as is to be seen in the extreme outward ex-pression. People who are never at home, who never sit still and meditate but must always be up and doing—or persuading themselves that they are doing—some-thing, who never can read quietly or listen to music or contemplate a beautiful prospect: these are the processives. They usually possess abundant animal energies and muscular or wiry frames, but their per-sistent activities wear them out and more tranquil types outlive them. The recessive type is emotional and sensitive; so imaginative that personal action seems unnecessary because it can enter completely into what it reads or pictures of the lives of others; it tends to be a recluse, dislikes travelling, new conditions, strange faces, and fresh problems, and never ventures far from home. It is shy, as the other class tends to impudence.

Mercury is usually regarded as a plus-minus quantity, convertible to either category, but thought is essentially a positive process—one cannot think nothing, nor can thought ever be stationary or recede; it is always an outward motion of the mind to consider something that is external to its own centre. Nevertheless, by reason of its universal and omniversal quality, by which it can equally well contemplate anything, Mercury is an intermediary in its action and assists to harmonize contraries. For, to understand an object, its right place must be found in the system of things and this is a process of reconciliation and adjustment. Mercury, however, does not alter things or alter itself; and if a real difference or contradiction exists, it can-not do more than discover its nature. To take an example, Mercury can disclose *why* Jones and Mrs. Jones do not agree, and if understanding were enough, this would naturally lead to reconciliation.

Venus is essentially the planet that makes compromises and will bargain for an equitable agreement, if Saturn is strong, or, if left to herself, will often give away her own position for the sake of quiet or even out of indolence. It must be constantly remembered that the field of Venerean action is far wider than that of sexual love or even of the affections as a whole; life is a constant adjustment and the whole of this process comes, at least in a general sense, under Venus. It is not strange, therefore, that she is the planet of happiness, for lack of adjustment implies a misfit, and a misfit implies irksomeness and irritation, even in the minutiae of life. Professional fighters, such as barristers or generals, always show their vocational scars in the form of Venus-afflictions, as we see, for example, in the case of Lord Birkenhead, who had the Moon in Libra in square to Mars and Venus herself opposed to Saturn. Mrs. Besant, a great orator rather than a debater, but also party to some important lawsuits, had a Libran satellitium afflicted in the 7th; and in Hindenburg's case there is the same group, showing military antagonisms. The list of generals with the Sun in Libra is a long one. Among combative politicians one thinks at once of the "Tiger" Clemenceau. It is incorrect to think of Sun–Aries or Sun–Scorpio as the great antagonistic positions; what rather seems to occur with these types is that they pursue their own road and only fight when someone bars the path. The willing fighter is Sun–Libra.

Nelson had this position; Wellington had Sun in Taurus.

An afflicted Venus seems, first and foremost, to be liable to signify an unhappy childhood. For a child has poor, because undeveloped, powers of self-adjustment. Children tend to be either violent or timid: in the former case they are checked and so made unhappy; in the latter case timidity is itself an unhappy state of mind. Next, a weak Venus is said to destroy conjugal happiness, making the native unloving, or else the victim of one that is. It is not good for associations with one's daughters or with any young girls. And, despite the attempts made nowadays (which are checked at every turn in practical astrology) to deny each planet more than one sign, Venus does rule Taurus and its connection with financial affairs is plain to see; hence its afflictions often manifest in this sphere.

Taken all in all, one is tempted to regard Venus as almost the most important planetary body and the one that alone makes life not only pleasant, but even possible.

Mars, on the other hand, is often dangerous to life. Yet he is a necessary part of the planetary scheme—as, indeed, we must believe to be the case with all the members of our system, difficult though it may be at times to think so. Mercury, with his rulership over the nervous system and its highest development, the brain, really makes man what he is—the thinker—and for that matter even natural intelligence, such as we see in animals and even in certain forms of vegetation, would be impossible without him. Without Venus life could never accommodate itself to its surroundings. Without Mars there would be no such thing as the individual, for, under the Venus influence, all things would tend to merge into one another and an undifferentiate condition would arise. Mars is the planet

51

that stands on its own, even at the risk of annihilation as the price of separation from the herd. When the Boers constantly trekked further into the heart of South Africa rather than suffer contact with, and interference from, alien peoples and customs, risking their lives at the hands of the natives, they were truly exemplifying the Mars spirit. The dislike of civilization, too, is Martian and it is this planet, rather than Jupiter, which drives people into the backwoods and implants the call of the wild. Jupiter, for one thing, is often social and at heart fond of comfort, so that, if it explores, it is generally pleased to return to cities after a while. Besides, the root-motives of exploration are different from those which cause people to settle far from their places of birth. All Martian characteristics may be traced to this fundamental impulse to preserve the self as a self, the misuse of the principle arising when there is undue sensitiveness on this point and a too egotistic and ruthless desire to insist on the personal life.

Jupiter is a constructive and progressive Mercury. The latter is concerned with things as they are; it examines, it does not speculate or plan ahead. Jupiter seems to be the type of the explorer and experimenter, always ready to sweep its gaze towards wider horizons whether mental or physical. It is always known as the planet of growth. This is not merely growth in the sense of a thing becoming enlarged; it is a perpetual unfoldment into fresh combinations and variations. The whole of Nature is an exemplification of this aspect of Jupiter—evolution is a typical Jovian manifestation and one of the most important. In the human being it is Jupiter which unfolds our possibilities and brings that which is latent into full expression: indeed, if self-expression is the purpose of life, then Jupiter, significantly the largest body in the solar system after the Sun itself, is the symbol of that purpose, the three prior planets representing principles which are prerequisites to this purpose. Life must have principles which maintain it before it can begin its main purpose. If it is correct, as here suggested, that Jupiter represents our life-purpose, then it is not strange that he has been named the "greater benefic," whilst the interpretation given above of Venus, as the factor upon which the maintenance of life depends, agrees with the title of "lesser benefic." And it will readily be perceived what a very deep and wide significance attaches to the position of Jupiter in the horoscope. Without its help we are necessarily destined to end, materially and intellectually, where we began. Jupiter is pre-eminently the planet of fresh contacts and new acquaintance. Venus is social, but it has a certain static element and does not seek fresh experiences; this is the province of Jupiter, and it is generally found that, if this body be strong, the native has many happy and fruitful associations with others, which are none the less profitable because the Jovian does not hold himself tied by them and constantly shuffles his friendships and his interests.

Saturn, it would seem, following the same train of thought, is primarily the planet that assimilates and consolidates what has been won. It follows upon two of the most progressive of bodies, of which Mars asserts, and Jupiter develops, the personality. But just as the self-assertion of Mars checks the mersive tendency of Venus, which would plunge our individualities into a common sea of alikeness, so it is needful that the desire to unfold that occurs under Jupiter should be held in check by the limiting action of Saturn; for, in finite nature, all things cannot expand perpetually. In fact, the very word "finite" brings us to Saturn and makes inevitable the presence of an influence such as his which sets a bound to things. But, as the opposite to the greater benefic, Saturn necessarily becomes the greater malefic, and, when his power is predominant in a horoscope so that the Jovian unfoldment cannot operate freely, he does actually become the stifler and thwarter of our radical impulses, the veritable enemy of life. One has only to see what happens when there is a late winter—the manner in which the deadly cold retards the outburst of Nature's springtime beauty to behold what Saturn can be. Exactly the same sort of thing happens psychologically, to follow the same type of Saturnine action, when austere parents crush the natural unfoldment of life and love in young children. On the other hand, households where Jupiter has been given unlimited sway and there has been no training or discipline of the young at all, are certainly equally unpleasant for visitors, though doubtless happy enough from the children's point of view. In a house of this character where it is considered wrong to check the children in any manner, the mother has Jupiter in Cancer in the 5th, conjunction Neptune and opposed to Uranus, a formation very indicative of chaotic and "unbounded" liberty. Saturn is in Pisces, introducing a similar note. Such people will think, feel, and do anything provided it is sufficiently unrestrained, indefinite, and indistinct. It is hardly necessary to add that they may be extremely likeable; in fact, Saturn seldom makes people liked; it makes them respected and causes others to rely on them when sound sense is needed. It is the planet of character and principle because these are (self-imposed) limitations—they limit what the native will allow himself to think and do and so consolidate his natural impulses into a definite system. Saturn is the least instinctual of the planets, being, in my view, far more distinctly human then even Uranus and Neptune; he is the body whose influence I find most difficult to see in animal-life, though it certainly appears in gregarious creatures, who associate and follow a leader. If man's task is to rise above his natural self and regenerate it, then it seems that Saturn is the highest of the planets in a moral and evolutionary sense, for the Saturnian man is furthest removed from the beasts. Indeed, one sometimes thinks that he would be improved by more impulse, by more animal spirit, by more natural *joie de vivre*. Mars often bestows the very courage which is needed to sustain the pain he inflicts, but Saturnians seem to derive most help from the idea of duty, so that the amount of satisfaction that a man obtains from the sense of having "done his duty" is some measure of the predominance of Saturn in his nativity. However, one needs to be very Saturnian in order to derive *pleasure* from the fact of duty performed, though most of us may find some consolation in this way, inasmuch as we all have some Saturnian element in our composition.

In relation to money, Saturn is interesting, for, contrary to what is often thought, he is not the planet of poverty, except in the negative sense that poverty is probable where he is weak. Saturn in the 2nd or angular, being also strongly configurated with the Sun, more often spells *property*, whereas the "fortunate" Jupiter frequently proves entirely disappointing in this respect. He, indeed, helps by often providing good friends and aid from influential people, but he is a free spender.[1] If one needs a supply of water it is not a swiftly flowing river liable to dry up suddenly that one requires, but a steady, though perhaps exiguous, brook, which can be partly dammed and will provide a dependable reservoir. So with Saturn. It may cause the inflow of money to be slow, but it is likely to be steady and to be well cared for when it arrives. Jupiter may save a little for the purpose of speculation, but it is no lover of prudent investment. Jupiter is usually well clothed on an overdraft; Saturn exemplifies the proverb that "many an old jacket has a good lining," and is always better off than he seems. The contacts of these two are naturally of great value from the standpoint of worldly position.

Uranus has suffered greatly, so far as true understanding is concerned, at the hands of the esotericists, who have attributed to him the most romantic characteristics. He is the magician in Holst's series, he is an adept, a superman, an occultist with a profound knowledge of what is hidden from the merely ordinary or Saturn scientist—it is so easy to have a great reputation if you can persuade others that it is of the essence thereof that your attainments are never to be demonstrated.

In ordinary life the Uranians I have known have not, as a rule, even faintly resembled this picture. One of their chief characteristics is a rough-and-ready unpolished manner, though this is less in evidence when the planet is in Libra, as may be supposed. They are very direct in their remarks, but to suppose that they are solitary eccentrics is a mistake. They are

[1] Lord Birkenhead, whose map has been given above, had ☿ lord 2nd. ☌ ♃, and he is said to have consistently overspent his income, enormous though it was.

generally sociable in their rough way, often good-natured and rather jolly people with plenty of fun and humour. It is true that they are eccentric, though many of their strange ways have become almost fashionable nowadays, e.g. vegetarianism, caravaning, discarding unnecessary garments, and so forth, but it is not necessarily a neurotic eccentricity. There is, in fact, a strong streak of the desire to get back to Mother Nature in Uranus, and, so far from being an adept with rigid self-mastery, he is often a rather untamed sort of person, thoroughly at home with the creatures of the woods. Wilful he certainly is, and he likes to have his way and can nourish resentments; but I do not think that the affections lack warmth; he is less detached than Aquarius and the appearance of many whom I have known does not suggest a Saturn relationship at all but rather recalls such a combination as Jupiter rising in Scorpio—dark-red complexion, dark or black hair, strong white teeth, a broad aquiline nose. The only pale Uranians known to me have had Saturn at least as strong as Uranus. The planet is *not*, as commonly believed, specially intellectual, though there is certainly always some tendency to an original cast of thought.

We have enunciated the theory that every planet represents a principle necessary to human life and unfoldment and we must now ask what is the significance of Uranus from this angle? It is usually said that, coming after Saturn, his task is to break up the too solid limitations that this planet has imposed. From the detached Mercury we pass to the conciliative Venus; from her who is so dependent on others we go to the individualistic Mars; from him we pass to the major series, crossing the gulf created by the planetary fragments, if such they be, called the planetoids. The major series starts with the progressive Jupiter and he is followed by the restrictive Saturn.

Do we now commence a fresh series with Uranus, first of the planets discovered in modern times? History seems to warrant this conclusion, for the discovery of Uranus certainly coincided with a rush of invention, social upheaval, and cultural development. One may mention the industrial revolution, the American War of Independence, which ended at Yorktown in the actual year (1781), when Uranus was found, the French Revolution, the blossoming of the Romantic school in poetry, and the beginnings of a huge scientific advance.

Uranus is known as the planet of originality, of freshness; and this expresses just what he is and why he is not, as has been supposed, a silent adept or a solitary, even in his commoner manifestations—why, in fact, his children are often breezy, fresh-complexioned, out-of-door people, as well as fresh in their ideas. He is the planet whose function it is to make us shake the dust off our feet and start afresh. How, then, does he differ from Jupiter and why does not the action of this planet suffice?

Jupiter, lord of double signs, is a paradoxical planet, fond of change and yet strangly conventional; one sees in him constant reminders of his being *within* the circle of Saturn's orbit. He may explore and hunt big game, but he is still hampered, from one point of view, by conventional limitations: one may rough it in Central Africa, because one *does* rough it there; but once back in London one reverts to the habits of London, without any question. Jupiter is growth—but it is always growth to a pattern set and approved.

Uranus is, then, the planet of originality, of the start

de novo. That is why it possesses considerable will-power or wilfulness; pioneers need that.

As for the love of power which is commonly attributed to the planet and which makes it, combined with other appropriate influences, a good governor and organizer, this may be ascribed to the same desire for originality, because power is needed to develop originality. Originality implies the overcoming of the forces of inertia and custom and this calls for power; as soon as Uranus begins to unfold his special function, he becomes conscious of this need for power whereby to do his work. If he cannot obtain it, in some measure, he is checked in his chief function and becomes the well-known Uranian rebel or Uranian neurotic.

Neptune remains the least understood planet, comprising as it clearly does something of Venus and something of Jupiter and therefore being related, by different authors, to Libra and to Cancer and Pisces, the two exaltation-signs of these planets. It is probably least of all like Mars and its influence on him is to soften and mitigate his violent tendencies, often with pleasing results, though should Mars, so to speak, get the better of Neptune, great cruelty may be found. Some writers emphasize the feminine character of Neptune and even seek to call him "her," others are as eager to stress his bi-sexual character. By some he is contrasted, as the Mystic, with Uranus, the Occultist. To some he is the Christ; to others very much the reverse.

It is certain that, from a material point of view, his aspects are often unsatisfactory. Many criminals and outcasts have Neptune strongly aspected, which seems to indicate their power of deceiving and preying on others. Neptune is often a sponger, with the further more creditable characteristic of being a free giver. He does not often improve the stamina of character or of body, and his children usually suffer from poor health; at best the physique is not robust. Sensitiveness seems to be his most marked characteristic and accounts both for the misery that he can cause, and for the artistic genius he often bestows. That he is more emotional than mental I cannot concede, for I have usually found that those with him in the ascendant are quite as intelligent as the average; in fact, such people have a sensitive mind, if not an acute one. Neptune rising in Gemini is unquestionably keen-minded. The possession of sensitivity also accounts for the kindness of Neptune, especially to animals. The influence of this planet is certainly as much in the direction of freedom and the Bohemian life as is that of Uranus, with the difference that Neptune has not the same rough vigour wherewith to pursue its own ways of behaving. A good deal has been written about both planets as being the symbols of universal love, brotherhood, and so forth, but I have never noticed that the natives of Uranus and Neptune are less individualistic than others; they are, however, less troubled by conventional forms, and Uranus in particular, does not care much about social distinctions; this, however, is hardly the same as being a practiser of universal love.

I cannot myself propose a more likely *raison d'être* for Neptune than the raising of man's sensitivity to a higher degree—in a word, the tuning of his reception to a higher pitch. *All* sensations mean more to the child of Neptune—witness his extreme dislike of noise. It would appear that, at the time Neptune was discovered, this added sensibility was (if we believe in a divine governance of the world) regarded as desirable. Not, of course, that Neptune had no effect upon mankind until he was discovered; in an individual sense he certainly was active in the case, for example, of James I, whose ascendant he occupied by transit at the time of the gunpowder plot; and when King Asoka founded hosiptals in India for man and beast he was probably actuated by Neptunian influence. However, the race as a whole has moved in a Neptunian direction since the planet was actually found, on September 23, 1846.

In one sense Neptune seems to be the opposite of Saturn, for he dislikes and tries to ignore or dissolve all boundaries and distinctions and, as a result, is often the planet of confusion, chaos, things lost and everything in its wrong place, and so he produces deception and illusion. It is well known that Neptunian action is rarely doing what it is supposed to be doing and that he often produces the fear of what does not come to pass. The man who said sorrowfully that he had spent much of eighty years of life in worry over what never happened, must have been the victim of an active but ill-placed Neptune. Furthermore, the illusiveness of Neptune is the very opposite of the concreteness and actuality of Saturn. The tendency that Neptune has to cause deception is hard to relate to the principle of sensitivity. It is part of the planet's other-worldliness and unwillingness to submit to the bonds of fact. Its imaginations are to it as real as fact; but to others this is not so, and they are deceived. Although we have a natural desire to sum up the natures of the planets under one idea which will express the heart of their significance, it is not necessary to suppose that this can now be done or ever will be done. Such an exact correspondence between ideas and actualities does not occur, and, though there may well be a primary meaning to each planet, there is nothing to suppose that there is one simple idea which expresses itself in numerous ways in each of them. After Saturn the planets certainly seem to become more complex in meaning. There is reason to suppose that, just as individuals, societies and nations have complete horoscopes, so a planet may have its nativity, in terms of other cosmic conditions at the time of its birth; and this nativity would express its significance, not in one term but in many. Hence the search for a single all-inclusive idea for each planet is probably vain and wrongly conceived.

Pluto was discovered in 1930, within the memory of even the astrologically very young. It is small, very distant, and has an orbit greatly inclined to the plane of the ecliptic, so that the attitude of those who deny its planethood is understandable. Those who maintain that it is a true planet can probably claim with right that it "works" astrologically; but when we ask them severally to give their votes in respect of its nature, we are met with considerable difference of opinion. This is evidenced by the suggestions that have been made as to its rulership. Its name has probably been responsible for the widely accepted view that it rules Scorpio, but others have strongly urged the claims of Taurus, pointing out that its discovery was synchronous with the beginning of the great slump of the years 1930–31–32 (this started in October 1929 and the planet was discovered in March 1930) and that the feature of this period was financial collapse, the breaking down of the exchanges, and the abandonment of the gold standard in Great Britain, the States, and other countries. Others have asserted that Aries is the sign ruled and Pluto has been described as a planet of self-assertion and publicity; Aquarius is also suggested. No doubt, as time passes and students have the opportunity to watch its effects closely as it meets directions in maps that they know well and have under careful observation, some reliable knowledge will be acquired. It is possible that the gloomy character implied by its name may not be wholly justified, and the most philosophic of astrologers may be pardoned for thinking that, after a series such as Saturn, Uranus, and Neptune, something to which the title of benefic can be applied without misgiving would not come amiss. It seems correct to relate Pluto to health and death and I have suggested that its nature is to bring to the surface, like a volcano or other eruption, what has accumulated unperceived over long periods. Thus it seems the planet of the "healing crisis." Death is often of this nature.

CHAPTER SIX

INFANT MORTALITY AND LONGEVITY

HEALTH is a subject by itself and one that could run
to several volumes so far as astrology is concerned. It
may be considered foreign to a work that is professedly
directed to the discussion of psychological problems,
but so intimate is the relation between the condition
of the body and the disposition, that it does not seem
out of place to devote a chapter to some of the
main principles that appear to underlie physical well-
being, so far as the horoscope is a guide to this. Ill-
health is liable to produce irritability, moodiness,
despondency, and even insanity; and on the other hand,
certain temperamental traits hardly ever appear in a
person who is fit in body.

The trick has sometimes been played on astrologers
of obtaining a lengthy delineation of the destiny of a
person who, it is afterwards revealed, died in infancy.

In a wide sense health is largely dependent upon the
preponderance of such life-giving and harmonizing
factors as the Sun, Venus, and Jupiter, over those of
an opposite nature. But Jupiter inclines to the running
of risks in health, as in all else, and Saturn, though not
a vitalizing influence, usually bestows a measure of
prudence that often justifies the proverb that the
creaking door hangs longest. Mars indicates, as a rule,
a tough constitution, but it certainly inclines to

infectious troubles, its ailments being generally infrequent but severe. Mars causes pain, Saturn weakness. Uranus is known to signify that the nervous system is often not normal and Neptune is a generally enfeebling influence, whose presence on an angle is very rarely indicative of vigorous health of body. The Moon, also, is too negative and receptive to be a beneficial influence in this respect.

It will be wise, however, instead of theorizing at length, to try to determine, as best we can, what the actual features of a natus of poor vitality are, for it cannot be too often insisted that constant speculative efforts, unchecked by an appeal to actual cases, has led astrologers in some instances very far astray. Referring to the table that follows, who would have signalled out Leo as being likely to occur as an ascendant most often of all twelve signs in maps of this category?

Tables based on few data have been criticized, but at least they are something better than mere conjecture, and when we get results, as in some cases below, that are nearly four times the average, we may safely conclude that we have a clue worth following.

In this table the slower-moving bodies are omitted, their sign-positions having no significance, or but little. Mercury and Venus naturally tend to follow the same frequencies as the Sun. The average figure for each planet in each sign being just over 3, we see that there are some striking maxima for Sun, Mercury, and Venus in Pisces, and for the Moon in Taurus. Some of the nil results are also interesting, such as Sun in Sagittarius and Moon in Scorpio.

Among the totals (average just over 22) Pisces alone is noticeably high, none of the others being much above

Table Showing the Positions of the Ascendant, Sun Moon, and Four Planets in Thirty-eight Cases of Infant Mortality

	♈	♉	♊	♋	♌	♍	♎	♏	♐	♑	♒	♓
☉	3	1	1	4	2	1	6	2	0	5	2	11
☽	4	9	1	4	7	3	2	0	1	2	2	3
☿	3	0	1	2	3	4	3	3	3	2	3	11
♀	3	3	2	2	1	5	1	5	1	2	4	9
♂	1	4	4	6	4	1	4	1	1	2	2	8
♃	0	2	3	6	1	1	4	2	5	6	7	1
Asc.	0	6	1	4	7	4	1	6	2	1	2	4
Totals.	14	25	13	28	25	19	21	19	13	20	22	47

66

the mean. On the other hand Aries, Gemini, and Sagittarius are low.

The most frequent ascending signs are Leo, Taurus, and Scorpio, but the excess over the mean is not enough to yield much certainty as to the significance of these figures.

Sun in Pisces is clearly the worst single feature 'as regards survival in infancy.

Total of bodies in negatives is one hundred and fifty-eight, against one hundred and eight in positives, i.e. nearly 50 per cent. more in the former, a difference too great to be ascribed to chance.

We come next to the more difficult question of the distribution in houses of the bodies in the same thirty-eight cases—a more difficult problem because of the differences of opinion that prevail in many quarters on the whole subject of house-division and, in particular, on the question of cuspal orbs, as they are sometimes called. As I have said in the Foreword, the present state of astrological opinion does not seem to justify any divergence from the usual practice of employing the semi-arc system and allowing an orb of 5° beyond the cusps.

The Campanus method is really useless for statistical work of this kind, because in it certain houses, i.e. those next the horizon, are on the average far larger than those adjacent to the meridian, the discrepancy being not so great in the semi-arc and Regiomontane systems. This, of course, is no argument against the merits of the Campanus theme, but it does mean that if we are to tabulate house-positions we cannot easily use it.

The average per house is 28½, so that the 5th is much below the mean, five bodies not occurring at all in it. The highest figure is for the 12th, just as Pisces is

Table of the House-Positions of the Sun, Moon and Planets in Thirty-eight Cases of Infant Mortality

	I	II	III	IV	V	VI	VII	VIII	IX	X	XI	XII
☉	4	2	6	2	0	0	4	5	2	1	7	5
☽	3	6	2	5	3	1	3	1	4	6	1	3
☿	1	6	4	1	0	0	5	5	2	3	3	8
♀	3	6	3	3	0	1	4	4	3	4	5	2
♂	5	2	4	2	0	1	4	5	4	4	5	2
♃	2	0	2	4	6	4	4	2	5	4	2	3
♄	5	0	2	2	0	6	3	1	4	5	5	5
♅	3	2	6	1	5	3	6	2	4	4	0	2
♆	4	1	5	4	1	5	0	3	4	1	4	6
Totals.	30	25	34	24	15	21	33	28	32	32	32	36

highest among the signs. The average occurrence of each body in each house is just over three and the highest figure is eight—Mercury in the 12th. In the previous table eleven occurred twice, so that either we are using an incorrect system or else house-position is less significant than sign-position. At all events, as a guide to the practical judgment of cases this table is a disappointment. We can probably say that bodies in the 5th, except Jupiter and Uranus, contra-indicate early death, and that bodies in the 12th, especially Mercury and Neptune, incline to it. Some beliefs, such as that bodies in the 6th and 8th are liable to cause death at an early age, must be regarded as severely shaken, if not disproved. Mars and Saturn are in the 1st ten times, against Venus and Jupiter five times, which supports tradition, but Mercury, for some strange reason—if it be anything more than chance— occurs only once.

It need not be pointed out that if we adopt the practice of some modern advocates of the Campanus and Porphyry methods and make the cusp the *centre* of the house, we entirely change these distributions, even if we retain the semi-arc system as our base.

As regards aspects, malefic contacts in mutables seem particularly dangerous, because they prevent the establishment of proper respiration. I have also noticed that in the great majority of cases we have one of the following conditions:—

1. Malefic in the 8th.
2. Malefic in close aspect to the cusp of the 8th.
3. Lord 8th severely afflicted by a malefic.

Sometimes the affliction to the cusp is by the lord of the house; this seems to operate destructively even though the lord is not a malefic. Retrograde malefics seem sometimes to fall within No. 2, even when in good aspect, if they are very severely afflicted. A case is that of a male, born 8.45 a.m., October 8, 1914, Geneva; died 9 p.m., May 1, 1915, at Geneva. Cause: broncho-pneumonia. Here condition No. 1 is almost fulfilled by Saturn, No. 2 occurs in respect of the retrograde and heavily afflicted Uranus, and No. 3 is very decidedly operative. Such examples could be very greatly multiplied.

Should we be right in supposing that the principles, such as they are, which we have asserted regarding infant mortality, are also valid as regards general health in later life? That is to say, for example, if Sun in Pisces is bad as regards infancy, would it also be bad later in life, if childhood were passed?

Presumably the same rules would hold good, except that there may be, and probably are, *some* positions peculiarly related to infant-mortality. Generally it is highly likely that a position that often goes with early death will also, when this is avoided, go with a weak constitution.

Probably aspects, which it is very difficult indeed to examine statistically, are immensely important; still, of the hundreds born on the same day, some must be strong and others weak, and yet, apart from the Moon, the zodiacal positions must be substantially the same. I have also known people who had far from good health although their maps were almost devoid of strong afflictions, whilst those with highly afflicted horoscopes sometimes do not suffer much in physical matters. It is plain from our tables that some positions are bad, whatever the aspects. Both Saturn and Neptune appear to be bad in the 6th and the 12th, and this is quite in agreement with experience. On the other hand I have known good health with Mars and Uranus in the 12th, but this is only what our table would lead us to suppose; the native (born August 1, 1878, Bournemouth, 8.0 a.m.) has Jupiter in the 6th, but the figures do not testify to that being a very useful position, though in principle it ought to be.

The alteration in the ascending degree and the aspects to it accounts for much variation in the health of people born near together, since a very few minutes can change these entirely.

The subject of longevity was treated very carefully in an article by A. G. Eames, appearing in *Astrology* for June 1932. His conclusions may be summarized thus:—

1. Many ☉ ♄ and ☽ ♄ aspects, including the □ but *not* the ☍.

2. ☉ ♃ and ☽ ♃ contacts (☌, ✶ and △, □ less common).

3. ✶, □, and △ contacts between ♃, ♂, and ♄; often all three are linked together.

4. All ☍ contacts are rare.

5. Afflicted ruler or ascendant or afflictions to the 6th and 8th houses are not serious unless all are weak. One strong one seems able to redeem the others.

6. ♀ usually strong.

7. ♃ in 8th very propitious.

8. In fifty cases of octogenarians, ♃ is ten times in ♊, only twice in ♐, eight times in ♍, once in ♓.

9. ♂ rises once but is setting in eight maps. He occurs eight times in ♋.

10. ☉ has the following outstanding occurrences: ♌ 6, ♈ 5, ♒ 8, ♍ and ♋ 6, ♉ 2, ♏ and ♓ 1.

11. ☽ has the following: ♋ 5, ♑ 8, ♍ 1.

12. Ascendant has the following: ♒ 1, ♌ 9, ♎ 8, ♑ 6.

13. ♅ and ♆ aspects do not seem noticeably helpful.

14. In sum, the main things are the relations of the Lights to ♃ and ♄; the mutual relations of ♂, ♃, and ♄; the 6th and 8th houses.

CHAPTER SEVEN

SUICIDE AND INSANITY

FROM cases of defective physical vitality we may now turn to those more strictly psychological instances wherein there is a primarily mental and emotional distaste for life and an unwillingness or inability to face it. In many of these there are unquestionably physical factors at work and it has been said that there has never yet been a suicide whose liver was in good order: nevertheless such examples will best be treated from a mainly psychological point of view. Suicide is often, of course, not the result of a general dislike of life; it may be due to some particular factor which has occasioned disgust and impatience. In all cases such maps are highly interesting, though unfortunately in most of them the details of the inner life of the victim of self-destruction are not on record.

It is an interesting commentary on the above quotation about the liver that a Jupiter–Saturn familiarity[1] is very common, if not almost always present, in suicide. Uranus is often considered the planet of self-destruction, but it is possible that this distinction may better be claimed for Neptune. It is true that the self-will of the former planet may incline to suicide; it has very little patience when thwarted. But its reaction is

[1] This phrase must be taken to include ♃ in a ♄ sign or ♄ in a sign of ♃.

more often one of anger; it is the planet of bad language. It may also indulge in a nervous breakdown. But it has recuperative energies, and fury is less likely to produce suicide than are the utter despair, debility, and misery that can come from Neptune, the effects of which are nearly always of an enervating and debilitating kind. When there are afflictions both of Saturn and Neptune, the way is difficult and the psychological condition abnormally sensitive. Saturn alone inflicts difficulties but gives a stubborn obstinacy that can endure; it is passively tough as Mars is positively so. Uranian suicide is the act of desperation; it occurs, but, it seems to me, not so often as the suicide of sheer wretchedness. A purely Saturnian suicide, if such there be, would probably be the result of material circumstances, such as poverty.

When Mercury is afflicted (as is usually the case) the mental state is probably unbalanced. If the afflictor is Uranus, one might usually diagnose insanity, but a familiarity between Mercury and Mars, such as is very common in these horoscopes, may indicate no more than mental rashness and the victory of impulse over thought.

Suicide does not always mean a very negative type of horoscope, but rather the reverse, for the suicide is not as a rule a person with no vital impulse, but with a powerful impulse that brooks limitations very ill. On the other hand, the very negative usually endures well and is feeble rather than rebellious.

A good example of the Uranian suicide is given below.

NATUS OF IVAR KREUGER

Native born March 2, 1880, Kalmar, Sweden. Data from *Modern Astrology*, see also *Astrology*, December 1933. Shot himself March 12, 1932.

SUICIDE AND INSANITY

Here there are no indications of an aversion to life, as such, but the strength of Jupiter points in the opposite direction. This planet, however, betrayed him. He was a megalomaniac of the insatiable kind with the desire

CASE No. 2

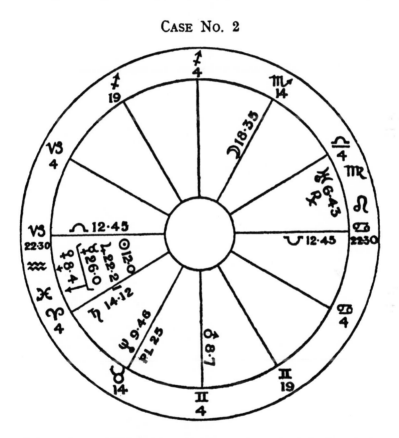

for wealth, which Saturn in the 2nd commonly bestows, developed to an abnormal degree. Given a certain amount of luck and the right sort of personality, any gambler may be successful for a time, and if he deals in huge sums, as this man did, he may reach a great height, especially whilst bull markets are prevailing over the world, as was the case in 1928 and most of 1929.

We shall constantly find a familiarity between the 8th house and ♆, even when the suicide is mainly of a ♅ character. Here ♀ ruling the 8th is in close square to ♆, the 3rd being involved. The contact is applying and I consider it the worst in the map and the one that was the condition precedent to his disastrous career. It showed, too, his Sybaritic tendencies.

♂, being angular, is the strongest planet, though at the nadir. It opposes the M.C. and effectually overthrew his position, as an explosion at the foot of a tower brings down the whole edifice, however lofty. It takes the squares of the ☉ and ♅ : here we have the element of desperation, which, in some form or another, nearly always occurs.

It is, of course, a weak map, as the maps of most of these so-called "kings of finance" are weak; there is nothing kingly about it. Only three bodies are in positive signs and the ascendant and five bodies are in the last zodiacal quadrant. We may refer to the passages in Chapter Four, page 43, treating of this form of unbalance; such people are never truly practical; they are dreamers and muddlers, whatever high pretensions they may make and whatever their sycophants may say about them.

If we take this map in terms of the signs, then we have ♄ ♈ as a 1st house influence—overweening ambition; ♆ ♉ as a 2nd house influence—shady finance; ♂ ♊ as a 3rd house influence—a rash and unscrupulous mind. The subterranean character of the life is shown amply by the fact that only two bodies are above the horizon, both in negative signs, and both lights, ☿ and ♃ (lord 10th) are in water.

We may now examine a rather exceptional case— that of a man who committed suicide at the advanced age of 80. Here the physical vitality must have been fairly strong and evidently survived the desire to live —the psychic vitality, as one might say, using this adjective in its strict sense. The motive for self-destruction is believed to have been general *taedium vitae*, rather than anything specific.

NATUS OF OCTOGENARIAN SUICIDE

Native was of the male sex and was born at Geneva, 11.30 p.m., May 16, 1831. He committed suicide by hanging (♄ strong by sign and aspect) at 11.30 a.m., September 2, 1911, at Geneva. I am indebted for this and other Swiss cases to the well-known astrologer of that nationality, Mr. C. E. Krafft.

Here the ☉ is closely configurated, in angles, with ♄ and ♆, whilst ♃ is in a sign of ♄ and in opposition to this planet. It is a nativity of sensitivity and sorrow rather than a desperate or wilful type, and it seems likely that loneliness, and perhaps the loss of the marriage-partner, ♄ being in the 7th, was the condition that precipitated the act.

Jupiter has been called a powerful help to those in trouble, and there seems no better testimony to its benefic influence than the fact that we repeatedly find its value weakened by Saturnian affliction in the maps of those who take their own lives. Where Jupiter has anything like normal play, there is too healthy a psychological state and too resilient spirits to allow of self-destruction. Mars also, though impatient, has much

77

combative force and likes to fight to the last; here he is cadent and debilitated by being in Cancer. Venus is hardly able to assist by reason of being without important aspect, as well as being cadent.

CASE NO. 3

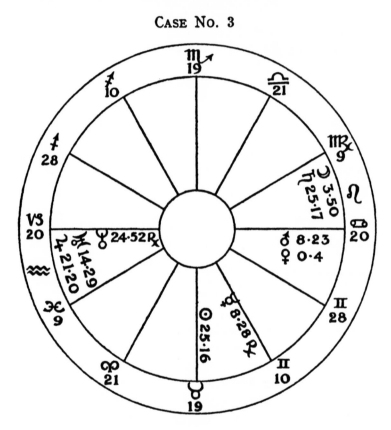

The fact that the two sensitive bodies, the Moon and Neptune, are both angular is in itself an indication of liability to mental and emotional suffering. But there is no sign of mental disease or disorder; it is a tragedy of depression pure and simple.

SUICIDE AND INSANITY

Three cases of suicide occur in my book, *Symbolic Directions*.[1]

Case No. 5 is that of a man who killed himself with poison in prison. ♆ is on the nadir, badly afflicted, but not in any familiarity with the 8th except that the ruler of that house, ☽, is in ♓. ☿ is in the same sign as ♂ but is not configurated with it. ♃ and ♄ have no familiarity. ☉ is ∠ ♆. The "element of desperation" is ☽ □ ♅. Data are 3.30 a.m., February 10, 1864, Geneva.

Case No. 6 is remarkable for many "good" aspects. Again the ruler of the 8th is in ♓ but hardly in aspect to ♆. ☿ is □ ♂. ♃ is in a sign of ♄. ☉ is ⚹ ♆. The "element of desperation" is not easy to find here, but there is the satellitium in ♈, well aspected though it is. Data: female, born 3 a.m., March 21, 1890, Geneva. Death by poison.

Case No. 8 shows ☽, ruling 8th, ⚹ ♆. ☿ is ☌ ♂. ♃ has no familiarity with ♄, perhaps here ♅ substitutes ♄. ☉ is ⚹ ♆. The ☿, ♂, ♄ formation constitutes the "element." Death by poison, male, born 11.15 p.m., April 9, 1900, Edinburgh. A cancer-investigator, one of twins. Discouraged by lack of funds and assistance.

If asked at this point for the chief indications of suicide, I should be inclined to say:—

1 ♆ in some relation to the 8th.

2. ☿ in familiarity with ♂.

3. ♃ in familiarity with ♄.

4. ☉ in familiarity with ♄ or ♆.

5. An "element of desperation" (often an ♈ group or a ♅ affliction.

[1] Those who have no invincible dislike of hypothetica planets may be interested in the positions of "Isis" in these three horoscopes, viz. No. 5—☉ ☌ ♏, No. 6—☿ ☍ ♏; No. 8—☿ ☌ ♏; all close.

Naturally all of these do not occur in every case, and the variety of reasons and conditions that lead to self-destruction is reflected in an equal diversity in the horoscopes of suicides. But three, at least, of these five will probably appear in most cases. We now give an example in which they are all to some extent represented.

CASE No. 4

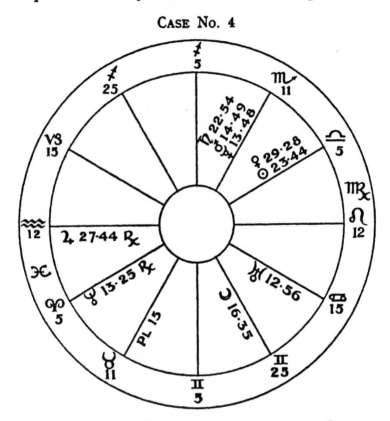

Female, born 2.30 p.m., October 17, 1867, Geneva. Poisoned herself 10.15 p.m., July 7, 1922.

Taking our five conditions, we find:—

1. ♆ is near 165° from the lord of the 8th.

2. ☿ is ☌ ♂ in a sign of ♂.

3. ♃ is □ ♄ in a sign of ♄.

4. ☉ is ☍ ♆ ; this is wide, but I have found wide ☌'s and ☍'s to be operative with the Sun.

5. The ♏ group, ☍ Pluto, constitute the element of desperation.

♆ is □ ♅ and ⚹ ☽, which I do not consider good. I have again and again found that so-called "good" aspects of ♆ signify nothing desirable, unless one can call the suicide's escape from life an act to be desired. Nor is ☉ △ ♃ always good; this, too, may make the native rather unfitted for life's rougher sides. It also may incline to some form of escape.

*　　　*　　　*　　　*　　　*

Melancholia is a state that has affinities with the suicidal propensity.

A case of the religious variety is given in *Notable Nativities*, No. 976. This is noteworthy for the combination of Saturn and 12th house influences. The Sun and three planets are in Aquarius in the 12th and Neptune rises in Pisces. The Moon and two planets are in Taurus, thus being disposed of by Venus, who is herself disposed of by Saturn. Jupiter is in Sagittarius only 4° past the meridian, and one might have hoped that this planet, being strong by sign and house and having ⚹ ☿ ♂ ☉, would at least give some hope amid delusion and foreboding.

CASE NO. 5

Girl, born in London, 4 a.m., January 11, 1903. Brilliantly clever. Suicide on December 26, 1930, without known reason.

Ψ is close to the cusp of the 8th.

☿ is △ ♂ (debilitated).

♃ is in a ♄ sign.

☉ is with ♄ in his negative sign and is also in wide opposition to Ψ.

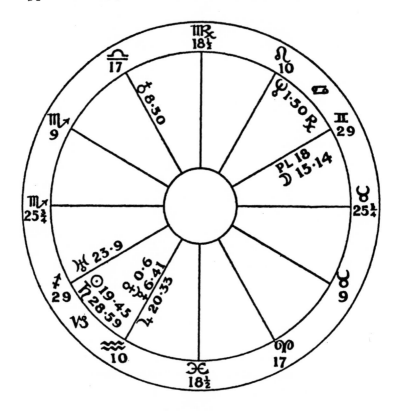

☽ with Pluto, ☍ ♅, constitutes the desperate element.

The position of Mars in Libra on the cusp of the 11th, in square to Neptune, involving the 7th and 8th, with the Moon, ruling the 8th, in the 7th, and Venus, the natural ruler of the 7th, in Aquarius in close conjunction with Saturn, indicates an attachment to a friend, probably older and in a different station of life.

Jupiter in the 3rd in trine to the Moon and Pluto in the corresponding sign sufficiently indicates ability, but Jupiter in good aspect to Uranus is also a testimony of like nature, apart from house-position.

Apart from these mental aspects, the map is difficult.

With this last example we will leave a tragic subject.

INSANITY

Among the horoscopic features of insanity may be enumerated:—

1. ☽, ♄, or ♆ angular; sometimes all of them.

2. ☿ in close ☌ with another body; this seems, in some circumstances, to strain the mind. It occurs in most cases that I have seen,

3. Planets in 23° to 27° ♊-♐, more rarely ♍-♓.

4. About 7° of the fixed signs, especially ♉ and ♏, seems to be a sensitive area.

5. Sun in aspect, not always afflictive, with ♆, less often with ♅.

6. The 3rd is afflicted either by the presence in it of a malefic or through the affliction of its ruler; more rarely a planet afflicts from the cusp of the 9th by "cuspal opposition," this last being more characteristic of mental deficiency than of insanity.

These rules throw light on a peculiar case published in *Modern Astrology* for September 1922. This was the map of a man who went mad in August, 1920, and set houses on fire. The data are: 3.13 p.m., June 29, 1898, 59.25 N., 5.16 E.

The positions are:

X	XI	XII	Asc.	II	III
♌ 29	♎ 1	♎ 23	♏ 8	♐ 6	♑ 15

☉ 8 ♋	☽ 8 ♏	☿ 7 ♋	♀ 11 ♌	♂ 16 ♉	
♃ 2 ♎	♄ 7 ♐ ℞	♅ 0 ♐ ℞	♆ 23 ♊	PL 15 ♊	

Orthodox astrology could point to the presence of two malefics in ♊ in the 8th as evidence of mental disease, and it could also indicate that the lord of the 3rd, ♄, is ☌ ♅ and ☍ PL, being close to the mid-point of these influences. But of these two conditions the former would be common to thousands of Scorpio-rising maps of that period and the second could hardly be deemed sufficient to account for so severe an outbreak. It would rather be expected to occasion some lesser form of mental peculiarity.

However, the first four of the above conditions are fully in evidence. No. 5 (☉ in aspect with ♆) is not to be found, unless we take 15° as a genuine aspect, as I am inclined to do. No. 6 is present, as we have said above.

We see from this that horoscopic circumstances that do not individually seem dangerous may become so, if they occur together and have a similar trend.

A second case is that of a girl, born in the West Indies, 8.0 a.m. December 30, 1903. Insane torpor from which she arouses herself to perform endless calculations.

The positions are:—

X	XI	XII	I	II	III
♏ 10	♐ 8	♑ 3	♒ 2	♓ 5	♈ 9

☉ 7½ ♑	☽ 17½ ♉	☿ 27 ♑	♀ 23½ ♏	♂ 14 ♒	
♃ 17 ♓	♄ 8 ♒	♅ 26½ ♐	♆ 4½ ♋	PL 19½ ♊	

Here ♄ rises in 8° ♒ and ☽ is also angular, so that Rules 1 and 4 are fufilled. ☿ is ☌ asc.—otherwise No. 2 does not apply. ♅ fulfils No. 3. Nos. 5 and 6 are obviously applicable—☉ ☍ ♆ ; ♂ lord 3rd. ☌ ♄ , □ ☽.

One of the saddest cases of royal insanity is that of the ex-Empress of Mexico, who lost her reason after her husband, Maximilian, had been shot by rebels. Her horoscope is in *Notable Nativities*, and is one of the worst imaginable. ☉, ☿, ♀ and ♂ are in the 3rd in ♊ and form a grand cross with ☽ in ♍ in 6th, ♅ in ♓ in 12th and ♄ in ♐ in 9th. ♆ in the 11th is in trine to ☿ ☉, but this only shows how little ♆ does to prevent evil; in this case he doubtless provided the best care for the unhappy widow, for ♆, even at the worst, often shields from *violence*. He is, in this instance, □ ♃ in the 8th.

CHAPTER EIGHT

THE VIOLENT CRIMINAL

IT is hardly necessary to speak of the potential importance of astro-criminology or to emphasize the interest the subject has always possessed for students of our science. It is, indeed, strange that no attempt has been made, so far as I am aware, to make a special examination of this field. We know that what are called afflictions may work out in many ways. They may, so far as can be seen, hardly affect the disposition at all, their whole operation being expended, as we say, circumstantially; or the reverse may be the case and the whole force of the afflictions may appear to turn upon the inner nature and corrupt it. There is a third alternative: both conditions may appear: the native may be violent to others and also the recipient of violence.

It would not be easy, I think, to separate correctly and at first sight twenty-four horoscopes, twelve of murderers, and twelve of murdered people.

I would say, however, that the most likely key would be the rising sign and the ruler. Moreover, in the maps of assassins it is rare to find *any* really good feature, though even here we must make exceptions, for a murderer may be the victim of impulse and may in many ways be a good man, superior, even in respect of kindness, to thousands who never break the law, but, without actual transgression, constantly and for years ill-treat others.

An example of one who suffered a violent end but was herself heroic and self-sacrificing is Edith Cavell. Her map is well known and is reproduced below;—

CASE No. 6

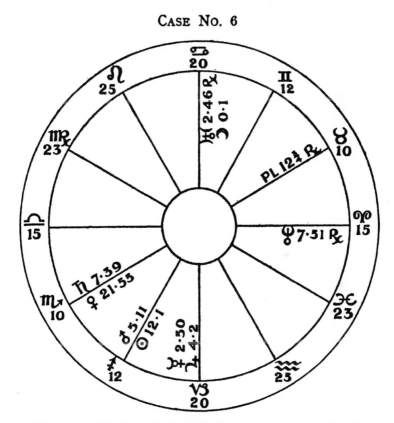

Nurse Edith Cavell, from *Modern Astrology*, October 1916. Born 2.30 a.m., December 4, 1865, Norwich. Shot by German soldiers in execution of a military sentence, October 1915.

Here there is a terribly violent configuration involving

the 3rd and 9th houses, and aggravated by the position of ♆.

But a gentle sign is rising, which, as we shall see, is rarely on the ascendant in maps of violent people, and four bodies—☉ ♂ ♀ ♄—are strong, or, at least, not seriously afflicted. One would certainly expect that Edith Cavell was highly-strung and perhaps at times self-willed and irritable from a purely personal point of view, but the rising Libra and, still more, the strong Saturn, subjugated all such merely temperamental things and gave the highest ideal of duty and helpfulness, with the courage to carry it out. It is an instructive horoscope.

Let us now consider the distribution of bodies in signs in maps of violent crime. This matter involves the Sun, Moon, and five inner planets. Owing to their slowness of motion it is not worth while to include Uranus, Neptune, and Pluto, which remain for long periods in the same sign.

Even the sign-position of the quicker bodies cannot afford such a precise indication as do aspects, and far less is it able to compete in this respect with mundane positions. For, since violent criminals are in a very small minority, it follows that the crucial astrological indication of a violent criminal must be something that lasts but a short time. Otherwise all the persons born on the same day, for instance, might be equally prone to a criminal career. Despite this obvious point one often hears some trait of character or fortune, and perhaps a very rare one, ascribed to a position of long duration which must necessarily be common to thousands of maps.

Thus we may regard all sign-positions as being of the nature of background influences, always excepting the rising sign, which is both a zodiacal and a mundane position, but is included here with the sign-positions. Without appropriate sign-positions there can be no criminal, but most assuredly all those who have them will not be doomed to crime. Temperament, indicated by the sign-positions, may incline them in that direction, but house-position, indicating circumstance, may save them. Aspects, the third consideration, may be regarded as midway between the two other categories and as representative of the interplay between temperament and environment.

The table that follows will be seen, upon examination, to give some very plain suggestions as to the main sign-positions that betoken a violent-crime nativity.

This table is highly instructive.

First of all, it is noteworthy that the three first signs, or first quadrant, contain no less than ninety-five "marks," as against forty-five, forty-seven, and fifty-one (a remarkably close result) in the three remaining quadrants.

This arises from the fact that the first signs tend (as we have said) to roughness and crudeness. Even their virtues are of the practical kind, but their vices are distinctly animal and tend to violent expression. On the other hand, the latter signs tend to be unpractical, idealistic, and vague, but are rarely ferocious.

♈ and ♉ total sixty-seven—against an average of about forty. This contrasts with ♌ and ♐ (or ♑) = 18. In other words, the worst pair is almost four times the best, whilst the worst sign, ♉, is more than four times the best, ♌. Such figures are very significant.

Even the ascendant occurs sixteen times in the first quadrant, as against seven, five, and six in the others;

TABLE I

Showing the Distribution of the Sun, Moon, and Five Planets in the Twelve Signs

	♈	♉	♊	♋	♌	♍	♎	♏	♐	♑	♒	♓
☉........	6	7	3	1	2	3	4	4	0	1	2	1
☽........	2	5	5	4	1	2	2	2	1	2	2	6
☿........	6	6	4	1	1	1	6	3	1	0	4	1
♀........	8	7	2	0	0	6	3	1	2	1	0	4
♂........	4	7	4	4	2	4	2	0	2	1	2	2
♃........	1	2	5	4	1	4	5	0	2	2	4	4
♄........	5	1	5	2	1	1	3	2	2	3	6	3
Totals.	32	35	28	16	8	21	25	12	10	10	20	21
Asc.	4	6	6	3	2	2	0	3	2	4	2	0

Thirty-four cases of violent crime have been used. Thus the average per sign per body is about three, and the average total for each sign is approximately twenty.

and this despite the fact that the first two signs are of very rapid ascension in Europe.

From ♊ (28) we fall heavily to ♋ (16) and yet more steeply to ♌ (8), this last being the lowest of all twelve. This may occasion surprise and many would expect ♌, as a fiery and passionate sign, to be higher than the sympathetic and cautious ♋. Figures, however, correct this expectation. ♌ is disclosed as a law-abiding citizen. The ferocity of the lion has, according to many, been grossly exaggerated, as also its courage.

The rise in ♍ and ♎ (21, 25) is surprising, for both signs have reputations for mildness. ♀ appears particularly evil in ♍, which one might anticipate, and ☿ and ♃ seem uncongenial to ♎, which one would not expect.

♏, the much-abused (at least by the ancients), provides a shock in its total of 12; and we see that ♂ and ♃ have not occurred at all in this sign.

♐ and ♑ are twins in innocency (10 each). ☉-♐ and ☿-♑ do not occur. Many would have expected ♐ to have been violent and ♑ avaricious and unscrupulous; but the figures gainsay this.

♒ rises to the average (20) and ♓ just passes (21). ♄ appears to be bad in the first and ☽ in the second, but ♀ in ♒ does not occur.

It must be admitted that many of these results are unexpected and seem to have no relationship with what is commonly understood respecting the psychology of the signs.

Perhaps the figures of the ascending sign are more in accord with *a priori* expectations. Despite their rapid ascension, ♈, ♉ and ♊ are high, whilst the slow-rising signs are low. ♎ and ♓ (both 0) live up to their reputations in this series.

Where the general teaching of this table is apparently not exemplified in a criminal map, I think it will be found that the violence has arisen from sensitiveness, or at any rate from some rather finer trait than brutality, lust, or covetousness.

We may summarize this table thus, using only the outstanding figures:—

Favouring violent crime:	Contradicting violent crime:
☉ in ♈ ♉	☉ in ♐
☽ ,, ♓	☿ ,, ♑
☿ ,, ♈, ♉, ♎	♀ ,, ♋, ♌, ♒
♀ ,, ♈, ♉, ♍	♂ ,, ♏
♂ ,, ♉	♃ ,, ♏
♃ ,, ♊, ♎	Asc. ,, ♎, ♓
♄ ,, ♈, ♊, ♒	
Asc. ,, ♉, ♊	

It is, of course, quite possible that an examination of, say, a hundred cases, would result in a considerable modification of the above. But it is probable that the figures given here, though based on so small a number of horoscopes, will afford a fairly reliable key to the problem with which they deal. At any rate the more striking variations in all likelihood point to the action of real astrological principles, and they also represent a rather powerful criticism of many of our traditional conceptions.

When we recollect that most, if not all, crime is really excessive individualism, or an act upon the part of the individual which ignores the rights of society and of other human beings, then it is fully in agreement with astrological principles that the first two or three signs should be heavily tenanted. For the first quadrant, or first three houses, has always been considered the most personal part of the map, and it is only to be supposed that the corresponding signs would have the same bias.

A preponderance of bodies in the first three signs and few or none in the last five or six is, then, a characteristic feature of the horoscopes of violent criminals. It cannot be said that this condition indicates violence as such, for the maps of those who commit violence from non-criminal motives do not always show this feature, though they sometimes appear to do so. On the other hand, it does not show criminality as such, for the non-violent criminal often has a fairly even distribution of planets and even at times satellitia in the later signs. This point is illustrated by such cases as N.N. 261 (adventuress), 391 (D. S. Windell), and 761 (defalcating bank clerk).

Are persons who have this preponderance necessarily inclined to criminality? It will be seen that the criminal map has other distinguishing features, but it may be true that all or most persons with many bodies in the first three signs are of the practical and even rough and rude variety, see N.N. 255 (collier, utter materialist, etc.).

The comparison of this table with that on page 20 of *Accidents* shows that in both of them ⊙ is high in ♉ and ☿ in ♈; otherwise there is no notable resemblance, so that, so far as sign-position is concerned, it appears that perpetrators of violence and victims of accidents can be differentiated.

We now pass to

The Distribution of Bodies in Houses

A table similar to that of sign-positions suggests itself. But actually such would hardly justify the trouble of compilation, because even with Placidus, and still more with Campanella, some houses tend to cover much wider stretches of the ecliptic than others. For example, the Campanus 10th, at London, can shrink to an area of about 8°, but the 6th can never contain less than about 27°, so that domal location is difficult to compare, except between opposite houses, which, of course, always have the same area.

However, it appears that the 12th house is very much more heavily tenanted than the rest, even allowing for its usually large area. It contains more than twice as many bodies as the 6th, for example. The 6th and 7th, though large houses (because adjacent to the horizon), are weakly held.

Other notable points are: ♂ and ♄ often rise, but ♃ never. ♅ in the 5th and ☉ in the 12th are common positions; indeed, ☉, ☿, ♀, and ♆ are often in the 12th.

The tables—like others based on small numbers—may be suggestive and they are compiled and published with that aim in view; they cannot prove anything. In fact, a statistician, accustomed as most are to employ many hundreds of instances in their work, would ridicule the attempt to extract anything valuable from so few cases. This, however, would be going too far; even in the examination of small numbers a very marked deviation from the mean, especially if it agrees with astrological principles, may be worth consideration and may point the way to something valuable.

Aspects

I have always affirmed my belief that the sphere of the Sun is action and its strength or weakness are, in the main, indicative of action successful or otherwise.

Tabulating the major solar aspects in our thirty-four cases and taking, in the case of the four malefics, the conjunction as well as the square and opposition as evil, whilst reckoning it as good in the case of ♃, and neutral in the case of ☽, ☿, and ♀, we have a total of thirty-seven major bad solar aspects against exactly the same number of good ones. ☉ ☌ ☽ occurs thrice, ☉ ☌ ☿ ten times, and ☉ ☌ ♀ seven times.

☉ in aspect to ♄ is most frequent, with a total, good and bad, of nineteen, whilst ☉ forms thirteen major aspects with ♂, fourteen with ♃, ten with ♅, nine with ♆, and twelve with ☽.

Note that in several cases the number of good aspects is swollen by trines that form part of grand-trine configurations, which the experienced astrologer would regard askance, even if he would not put them down as positively evil.

The lesson to be drawn from the equal number of good and bad aspects seems to be that criminals such as we are examining usually have a severe solar affliction, there being thirty-seven such among thirty-four maps, but that they often have good aspects to ☉ as well; this perhaps shows their skill in action, daring, and other good qualities which, apart from the purpose to which they are put, would be admirable. Probably the number of good aspects to ♄ (ten) will be the most surprising element in this tabulation.

A similar examination of lunar aspects yields a much more interesting and, in fact, an almost startling result.

These may be stated thus:—

Moon	Total Major Aspects	Good	Bad
In aspect with ☿	11	10	1
,, ♀	11	7	4
,, ♂	10	4	6
,, ♃	17	17	0
,, ♄	15	3	12
,, ♅	16	6	10
,, ♆	14	6	8
Totals	94	53	41

Here we find considerably more aspects than are formed by ☉, although ☽'s aspects only comprise those made to seven bodies, whereas in the solar lists aspects are formed to eight, ☽ being in that case included. And instead of the number of good and bad aspects being equal in number, there is a preponderance of the former of about 25 per cent.

In particular, against twenty-seven good aspects formed to the two mental planets ☿ and ♃, there is but *one single affliction*, a truly noteworthy result.

On the other hand ♄, and to a less extent ♅, is more often in affliction with ☽ than in good aspect, whilst ♂ and ♆ do not show great differences. ♀ is more often in good aspect, and ☽ △ ♀ in water seems rather frequent.

We come now to ☿.

Having already tabled the aspects of this planet to ☉ and ☽, we have the following figures:—

Mercury	Good	Bad	Total
In aspect to ♀	5	0	5
,, ♂	4	10	14
,, ♃	5	4	9
,, ♄	5	2	7
,, ♅	5	8	13
,, ♆	3	5	8
Totals	27	29	56

The outstanding figures here are, of course, those involving ♂ and ♅, and I may add that it is, to say the least, most difficult to find a map of the class now under study that does not contain a relationship between ☿ and ♂ or ♅. Sometimes this arises through the signs, ☿ being in ♈ or ♏, or ♂ or ♅ being in ♍ or ♊, but most often a bad aspect is in question.

Coming now to the aspects of ♀ we find that there are approximately equal numbers to ♂, ♃, ♄, ♅, and ♆, and that, moreover, the difference between the number of good aspects and bad ones is insignificant, both as regards the totals (24 good, 25 bad) and in regard to each planet.

However, it is to be remarked that where ♀ has good aspects, these are often spoilt by her being in debility (particularly in ♈) or by the planet to which she is in aspect being so.

Venus seems to suffer debility, at least so far as our present investigation is concerned, more from being in ♈ than from being in ♏. She is also weak in ♍.

It hardly seems possible to say that any specific afflictions to ♀ occur in all criminal maps, but there are probably very few exceptions to the rule that this planet is never strong. In aspect to ♆, financial dishonesty—or at least muddled finances—is implied, and though we are now dealing with violent crime, it is plain that one thing may easily lead to the other. This seems to be the case in Angerstein's life (see page 100).

♂ is often in relation to ♃, usually by conjunction or by bad aspect, sometimes by a good aspect spoilt by weak sign-position, and sometimes by the presence of one planet in the sign of the other. Cases in which there is no connection at all are in a minority. Probably this circumstance is due to the courage and resource that the mutual influences of these two bodies usually signify.

In about half the cases there is a major bad aspect between ♂ and one or more of the four outer malefics, but in some cases ♂ seems to have no severe affliction.

The aspects of ♃ to ♄, ♅ and ♆ are comparatively few in number; possibly they tend to occur more frequently in the maps of a higher order. Curiously enough there is some evidence that the benefic aspects are the commoner. With ♄ there is a conjunction, one good aspect, and three bad ones, but with ♅ there are two conjunctions, six good aspects, and three bad ones, and with ♆ there is one conjunction, seven good aspects (sextiles specially common), and only two good ones.

From such meagre figures one cannot venture to say that ♃ in good aspect to ♆ favours violent crime, but one is certainly justified in declaring that the data prove decisively that his position does not deny it.

The same is true of the lunar figures given above; impressive though they are, one cannot perhaps say that ☽ △ ☿ and ☽ △ ♃ *cause* crime, but one can most definitely state that they do not prevent it. And this is an important assurance, for very many astrologers, guided or misguided by too great reliance upon partially understood principles, would probably say that the second, if not the first, of these aspects would be productive of honesty and dependability.

I confess myself quite unable to explain why such configurations are common and it is because surprising results such as these are produced by statistical research that the latter is so valuable.

The mutual aspects of ♄, ♅, and ♆ are formed too slowly and endure too long for it to be possible to derive useful information from an examination of their frequency.

To me a bad aspect between ☿ and ♂ suggests an impulsive and violent temper, whilst one between the same planet and ♅ implies a mental kink and is more allied to insanity. A case in illustration is that of the German Angerstein, dealt with in *Astrology* for spring, 1928.

CASE No. 7

"Below is the natus of a German named Angerstein, who was born on January 3, 1891. Details are taken from the *Astrologische Rundschau.*

"The native was a departmental manager of a large chemical works. He had always enjoyed great respect and had passed for a good citizen and a religious man. Between November 29th and December 1st, 1924, he killed eight persons, in part relatives and in part subordinates. It is believed that he had previously killed his wife, mother-in-law, and maid. He killed his young sister-in-law, who returned late on the Sunday night. On the next day he accounted for two gardeners and two employees. In order to extinguish all trace of his deeds he set his house on fire, gave himself a wound, and ran shouting for help to his neighbours, declaring that he and his family had been attacked by murderers. However, the police unmasked the real state of affairs, and placed Angerstein in a clinic under medical

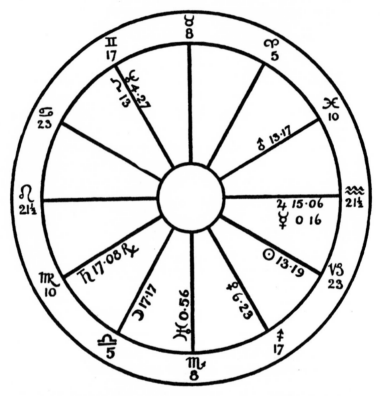

observation. It appeared that he had misappropriated fairly large sums."

(From *Astrology*.)

Here the sign-positions are not criminal, but there are certain aspects which have that tendency, e.g.

☽ △ ♃ and ☉ △ ♄, which we have noted,[1] and ♀ ☍ ♆. However, I should blame ☿ □ ♅ for the tragic outburst and would judge that there was here something of the nature of mental instability, although one could, perhaps, not go so far as to say that the native was insane. Heavy afflictions in mutables are sure to affect the mind, but insanity is usually, if not invariably, indicated by much heavier afflictions.

In many respects this is a good horoscope, with something dignified and unusual about it that is extremely attractive. But there is a heavy concentration, or focus, upon the 3rd house. ♊ contains two afflicted malefics, ☿ itself is afflicted from the 3rd (for ♅ must be definitely placed in the 3rd, despite the modern theory that would make it a 4th house influence), and the ruler of the 3rd is afflicted. This was indeed a strong attack on one point.

Pluto is in 6 ♊.

CASE NO. 8

"Our next example is the nativity of another German (born October 25, 1879), and named Haarman, and is also taken from the *Astrologische Rundschau*.

"The details hardly bear translation. He was a weak-minded homosexual maniac, who passed considerable periods in asylums and prisons, being also convicted of theft. Finally he was executed (April 15, 1925) as being guilty of the death of about 27 young people, mostly boys of from 16 to 18 years. These murders appear to

[1] Such aspects as these may be bad in the sense that they give some success and responsibility and therefore expose the native to temptations to which he would not be subject if he had nothing but bad contacts. This seems to have been the case here.

have been committed in 1923 and 1924. He stated that his own condition was a riddle to him; he was diseased, and would do again what he had done, if he were liberated; he had no wish to go to gaol or asylum, and asked that he might be 'set free' by being put to death,

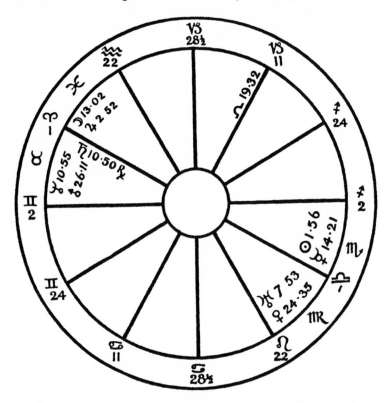

saying that death was only an operation and lasted but a moment.

"This man's condition was certainly more radical than that of Angerstein and more thoroughly unbalanced. Consequently we are not surprised to find a very different style of horoscope, and, to begin with, a much more plebeian one. Every planet except Saturn is in a negative sign, and four houses contain all nine bodies, as well as the Part of Fortune."

(From *Astrology*.)

Pluto is in 26¾ ♉.

This points to a sordid type of mind, or at least one that is at a low state of unfoldment.

The horoscope is no more promising when reviewed in the light of our inquiries. Five points are badly placed zodiacally (☽, ♀, ♂, ♄, and asc.) and there are no good sign-positions. The 12th is heavily tenanted. ♂ rises and ♅ is in the 5th; ♆ is in the 12th.

There are three aspects that fall within those we have stigmatized as ominous, viz. ☽ △ ☿, ☽ ☍ ♅, and ☿ ☍ ♂ (very wide). Observe that in the case of the suicide and swindler Kreuger we had ☽ △ ☿ in the same signs, though reversed. There was much cunning in both cases; each knew how to lure his victims to their fate.

17° of the mutables is an area often occupied in the maps of those who suffer judicially. Angerstein has ♄ in 17° ♍ and it is noteworthy that he and Haarman both have bodies in 13° ♓. In the case that now follows (from *Astrology*, June 1931), ♅ is in 19° ♍.

CASE No. 9

The native was born at 3.30 a.m., May 26, 1883, at Cologne.

He was a kind husband and a good workman, but, side by side with these amiable traits, he was a man devoured with a lust for blood and an ambition to excel all known assassins in his widespread feats of destruction. He served terms of imprisonment for theft and arson, having been brought up under very untoward conditions, but his wife stated that on one side he was gentle, inoffensive, and sympathetic; he struck her only once and then apologized, promised

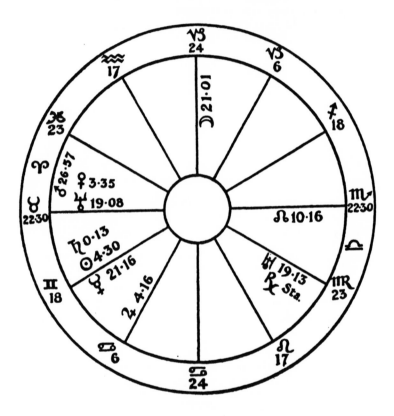

never to repeat the act, and kept his word. Yet there was always this bitter resentment against mankind, and, in particular, against women. He was known as a German Jack the Ripper, his murders being associated with sexual depravity.

THE VIOLENT CRIMINAL

The natus is highly interesting. A primitive type is clearly hinted at by the presence of the ascendant and seven bodies (including Pluto, in 29¾ ♉) in the first three signs. The ruler and Mars are in the 12th, showing the imprisonments, and Neptune, associated with the 12th, is rising. Saturn, Pluto, and the Sun form a terrible satellitium in the 1st house; the grand trine of the Moon, Uranus, and Neptune probably indicates the gentle side of his nature, but it was corrupted, so to speak, by the impact of two squares— Mars square the Moon and Mercury square Uranus, the one brutal, the other apt to give just that fatal twist to the mind that ruins whatever of promise the map otherwise contains. We have seen it already in Angerstein's case, and it can be found often enough in criminal horoscopes. Uranus in the 5th accounts, to some extent, for the sexual outrages, yet the strength of Venus makes it difficult to account for these. Her heliocentric position, however, is in opposition to Uranus, which provides a case in favour of the value of this class of co-ordinate.

Jupiter may appear something of a problem, whether he is to be regarded as a 2nd or a 3rd house influence, or indeed, as affecting both houses. But in the 2nd he inclines to carelessness about money or at any rate a free way of handling it, and this position is quite possible in a poor man's map. In the 3rd he tends to produce self-satisfaction, and there is no doubt that Kuerten experienced a diabolical joy in contemplating his achievements and in planning fresh and ever more terrible feats of bloodshed. Jupiter in Cancer is emotional, and the sensational part of the disposition is easily stimulated.

The native was condemned and executed.

CASE No. 10

This is the natus of Leggs Diamond, the gangster who tried to evade his enemies by flight to Germany but was turned back and killed, dying penniless. Born at 2 a.m., July 10, 1897, at New York.

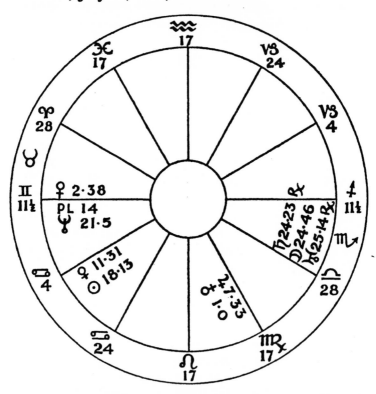

Primitivity appears in the asc. and seven bodies in the first half of the zodiac, and still more in the forbidding Scorpio satellitium in the 6th □ ♂. Aspects are few and bad, ⊙ △ ♄ (wide) being almost the only good contact in the map. The asc. indicates a quick mind and hand, and a handsome, plausible appearance. The Sun is in an area connected with finance (see notes on Rhodes' and Rockefeller's maps in the next chapter). The very phrase "under-world" suggests Pluto and the daring nature of the game at which the native played bears out, to some extent, those who attribute a Scorpio affinity for this planet.

CHAPTER NINE

OUTSTANDING ABILITY AND FAILURE

ONE of the most difficult things to determine, at first sight, is the mental capacity of the native. We begin our astrology with the belief that we have only to examine Mercury in order to decide this important point; but we soon discover that this, by itself is hardly any clue at all. I have seen cases in which this planet is brilliantly aspected and there has been no particular strength or depth of intellect; only readiness at retort and a certain amount of shrewd sense.

The "cross" formation seems to make for mental ability. In cardinal signs there is usually a vigorous, active mind, and in mutable signs a versatile and highly intelligent one. In fixed signs there is rather a tendency to brute energy and courage. But if we look through a collection of nativities of persons who have achieved distinction in some intellectual or artistic vocation we are struck by the variety of types of astrological formation that we encounter. It would seem as if we must accept the Platonic teaching that all souls possess, in a latent manner, all knowledge, but that outstanding ability is manifested when a soul obtains a suitable environment—suitable, that is, to the expressional urge of that particular soul. In all other cases there is not a lack of genius, but a failure to encounter just that concord between inner genius and exterior circumstances that is a necessity if the former is to find expression in the world.

Either Sun or Mercury in good aspect to Uranus or Neptune—these occur frequently in the maps of geniuses; but Jupiter is also important, as might be expected, in this regard, and not only the Sun or Mercury in good aspect to him, but, in particular, Mars sextile, trine or conjunction Jupiter is, as research will disclose, very common. However, none of these contacts constitute a guarantee of great ability. They are fine tools, but, to revert to our Platonic point of view, they may not be the tools that the particular ego can use or wishes to use, and in such a case they will produce comparatively little.

Certain fields of expression are appropriate to each planet and, astrologically, every planet is a faculty for work in an appropriate direction. For example, one might say that Mercury excels in commerce, Venus in art, Mars in engineering and reformative works, Jupiter in religion—which, to an astrologer, is a faculty like love of music, Saturn in philosophy, ethics, and government, Uranus in organization, Neptune in music and the drama. But there are countless subdivisions of planetary activity.

It may be instructive to run through a certain number of cases of well-known men to whom outstanding abilities of a mental order can be ascribed and to see what are the *main* features which in each case indicate the possession of unusual faculties. In each there is likely to be an outstanding aspect, sign-position, and domal influence.

1. Marconi (see *Astrology*, March 1930).

Born 9 a.m., April 25, 1874, Bologna.

(a) ☿ △ ♅, ☽ △ ♆, ♀–♂ △ ♃.

(b) Heavy ♋–♉ concentration—natural science?

(c) Many bodies in 11th, corresponding to ♒—science.

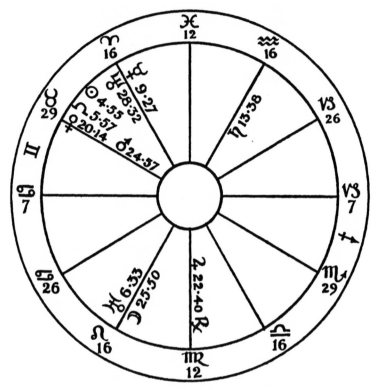

2. J. D. Rockefeller (*Modern Astrology*, April 1930).

(a) ☉ △ ♅, ♂ ☌ ♃ △ ♆, ☿ △ ♄.

(b) ☉ in degree-area of ♋ signifying wealth.

(c) ♄ angular, a common condition in maps of successful accumulation.

3. Pasteur (N.N. 950).

A fine example of the map of great mental powers.

(a) ☉, ☿, ♀, ♅, ♆ in ☌ △ ♄, ♂ △ ♃.

(b) As in Marconi's case the earth-triplicity is

strong, containing eight bodies, the ninth (☽) being in ♊.

(*c*) The ♑ bodies are concentrated in the 3rd.

This is a map unusual for its lack of contactual affliction, so common in maps of great mental proficiency.

4. George Washington (*Astrology*, March 1932).

Born 10 a.m., February 11, 1732, U.S., at Bridges Creek, Virginia.

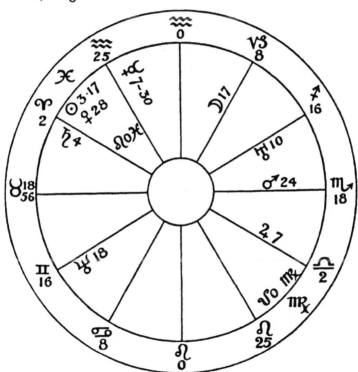

(*a*) ☿ △ ♃, ✳ ♄ ♅.
(*b*) ♂ angular and strong by sign and aspect. But the map is not that of a natural militarist. The

native owed much to ☿ angular and in exact
△ ♃; he was intelligent; his opponents were not.

5. Cecil Rhodes (N.N. 318).

   (*a*) ☉ ☽ ✶ ♅ △ ♆, ♂ ☍ ♃, ☿ ✶ ♂.

   (*b*) ☉ is near Rockefeller's and the Cancer–Taurus positions are indicative of wealth. Ruler exalted.

   (*c*) Five bodies angular.

6. Baden Powell (N.N. 837).

   (*a*) ☽ ☿ ✶ ♂ ♃, ☉ △ ♄, ♀ in 3rd ⊻ ♅, ♆.

   (*b*) The blend of end-zodiac and beginning-zodiac signs is good for carrying idealistic work into action.

   (*c*) Four bodies are angular.

7. General Ulysses Grant (N.N. 237).

   (*a*) ☉ ♄ ♃ △ ♅ ♆, ☽ △ ♀; but ☿ has only a weak □ ☽ and △ ♂, being also cadent. Not the map of an intellectual but of a genius in a certain fashion.

   (*b*) Note the same rising sign as Washington; Venus influences are often prominent in military maps.

   (*c*) Four angular bodies.

8. Bismarck (N.N. 254).

   (*a*) ☉ △ ♅ ✶ ♄; ♂ △ ♃; ☿ ✶ □ ♆ (secret diplomacy).

   (*b*) The bodies are well distributed.

   (*c*) A strange lack of angularity for a man so prominent in his generation. Is the time authentic?

9. Isaac Newton (N.N. 739).

   (*a*) ☉ ✶ ♅ ♃ ♄; ☿ □ ♃ ♄; ♂ ✶ ♃.

   (*b*) There is a distribution tending towards the

last six signs, showing the man of thought and ideas rather than of action.

(c) ♀ ♂ angular.

10. Mussolini (*Modern Astrology*).

    (a) ♆ △ ♅ and ♀ ♃ ✶ both; ☉ ☿ ✶ ♄ ☽ ♂.

    (b) A strange concentration in three successive signs.

    (c) Five bodies are in or close to angular houses.

These maps give a good idea of the kinds of aspects from which we can expect some unusual manifestation of ability. Some people seem to owe more to house-position. For example, Lord Northcliffe had Mars (according to the generally accepted time) on the M.C. ✶ ♅. Gladstone had Uranus close to the same angle, ✶ ☉ ☿. Ramsay MacDonald has ♆ there, ☌ ☉ □ ♂ ♅ △ ☽ ♀. Helen Keller has ☿. Indeed, a planet close to the M.C., strongly aspected, inclines very much to fame, and if the Sun and Mercury are also strong, so as to give general abilities and good sense, the native may go far. But *close* proximity is very important; one may question, for instance, whether Gladstone actually had Uranus as far as 4° from the meridian.

A good case of the determining power of planets in the M.C. is given below.

CASE No. 11.

A boy born at 9 a.m., January 6, 1920, Ma-u-bin district of Burma.

This boy developed at the early age of five into a preacher who attracted thousands to listen to him. Special boat- and train-services were run to enable the crowds to attend his discourses, which were Buddhistic. His parents are peasants. He answers all questions put to him by the priests with the utmost readiness, and claims to be the reincarnation of an abbot. It is said that he abhors females, and also gold, silver, and other precious things; in disposition he is imperious and wilful.

Here ♀ in ♐ is characteristically on the M.C., whilst

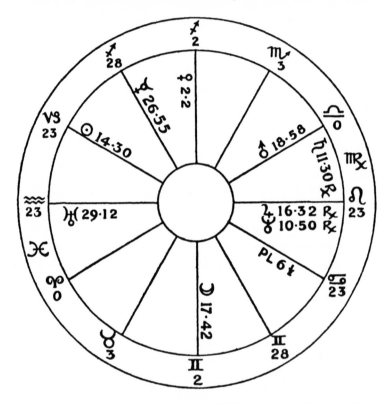

we have ☿ ✶ ♅, and ♂ ✶ ♃ ♆. Wilfulness is denoted by ☉ □ ♂ but ☉ is also △ ♄. Mental ability is well shown by the angular ☽ in ♊, with several strong good aspects.

It has been mentioned that strong aspects of stress often produce mental powers of an exceptional character, but they are generally wrongly or unwisely employed, or lack opportunity, according to the special nature of the afflictions.

In this case ♅ is in square to ♀ and ♄ to ☽, though wide, and this indicates the celibate life of the Sangha, which the boy intends to enter.

It would seem that most infant prodigies have maps that are not superficially attractive, as if the premature unfoldment of their powers were the result of some special stellar stress. I have the case of a boy born at Brighton, just after midnight, October 30, 1917; he is very musical but is in fact far ahead of his coevals in all subjects, always getting to the top of a form as soon as he is put into it.

Here there is an opposition 3rd to 9th, squared from bodies in Leo rising.

The exceptional brilliance is shown by Jupiter in Gemini trine the cusp of the 3rd, and by Venus, ruling that house, in close sextile to Uranus; no doubt Neptune, though afflictive, is also in part responsible, especially for the musical gift.

This map well illustrates the importance of the 3rd from the mental point of view. A powerful 3rd, showing one who lives in the mind, will often go far to supplant the ascending sign as the most active part of the personality.

A girl born at London, 1.34 p.m., January 8, 1911, became well-known and highly successful in her early 'teens as a designer. Her nativity is a remarkable one; seven bodies being in cardinals. Mars is exactly setting; note that he is in mutual reception with Jupiter, whilst our other suggested contacts are well represented (☉ ☿ ♀ ☌ ♅ ☍ ♆, etc).

But sometimes the prominence of the 3rd is to some extent veiled. The natus of the learned Dr. Garnett, Keeper of the Books at the British Museum and writer on astrology under the anagrammatic name A. G. Trent, has nothing in the 3rd, though his life was so occupied with books. But Jupiter in Gemini is close to the M.C., trine Neptune. Mars, ruling the 3rd, is trine Uranus, Sun, and Moon, and is in the 10th.

In this map there is a good example of what I call *domal analogues*, or powerful correspondences between points in the ecliptic and in the mundane sphere. The ascendant, 12½° Virgo, is two-fifths of the way through the sixth sign; now, if we take a point two-fifths of the way through the 6th house, we get exactly to Uranus. This transfers something of the Uranian influence to the ascendant and, be it noted, the planet is in an astrological area. But this alone would hardly account for an interest in astrology, especially in one brought up in mentally orthodox circumstances and born under as conventional a sign as Virgo. The transference of Uranian influence from the obscure 6th to the ascendant enables the more original vein to appear.

In this map there is a like relationship between Mercury and Saturn, which we should certainly expect to be related in some way to the mental planet.

These analogues are important when close, and, since they change rapidly with the ascendant and other cusps, they serve to differentiate maps otherwise alike.

Note in this map the preponderance of bodies in the last signs.

*   *   *   *   *

Some thought may now be given to the unsuccessful map, or the horoscopic characteristics of the complete failure.

Non-success may, of course, be due to conditions that are hardly psychological, such as physical ailment; and this might be indicated by one strong adverse aspect, so dominant as to thwart all else in the nativity. But such a case as this is not true failure; unless the native accepts defeat as the necessary result of his state of health, there is no defeat, and even the most afflicted person, by resolute cheerfulness, may turn a worldly reverse into a psychological victory. For this last consists in a twofold action: Alteration of adverse conditions where this is possible and adaptation to them where it is not. In few words,

> For every evil under the sun
> There's a remedy or there's none;
> If there is, find it out;
> If there isn't, do without.

Or, in Stoic language, "he hath an understanding of things divine who hath nobly agreed with Necessity." Psychological success, then, unless we are fatalists, is within the power of everyone.

It is the failure to make *anything* of life that is real defeat.

This would most commonly correspond to a horoscope that lacked integration, i.e. few aspects and weak ones. Such a person drifts and can (apparently) make no effort to aid himself or to respond to those who would assist him.

Heavy concentrated affliction may also suppress self-expression, as in mental deficiency—but this is not so much failure as absence of a real attempt at living, owing to the obstacles presented by the physical body.

Lack of balance will often indicate failure, generally through a psychological foolishness or ineptness, which makes the native unable to respond in a spirit of commonsense to his environment. I have known such a case: Mars rises in Capricorn, sextile Jupiter in the M.C.; a satellitium in Aquarius in trine to Saturn in Libra; Sun in Pisces, trine Jupiter but square Uranus:

this and a square between Mercury and Jupiter were almost the only afflictions, unless the grand trines between the bodies in air be counted as such. The bane of the native, besides the quarrelsomeness of Mars, was the day-dreaming propensities of air, augmented by the Sun in water. Despite the reputation of Capricorn for practicality, the native was the most unbusinesslike of men and could never carry out the simplest operation in an efficient manner. Moon in Aquarius is often inefficient. This man was ambitious and very energetic, but had no sense. Many would have regarded his nativity as a brilliant one, and one must allow that it seems strange that he was not even the recipient of fortuitous good fortune. In this map only two bodies—Neptune and Uranus—were in the first six signs.

Extraordinary luck would seem to be the gift of good aspects of Jupiter, Uranus or Neptune. Sometimes both good and bad luck seems to be derived mainly from domal positions, and one is reminded that the Greeks called the 11th and 12th houses the good and bad "Angels" respectively. Calvin Coolidge became President of the United States through what was, from his point of view, accidental, and his presidency coincided, through no merit of his, with a period of great prosperity. His map, however, does not seem conspicuously lucky, except that the 11th is heavily tenanted.

Data are:—

Born 9 a.m., July 4, 1872, 43.35 N., 72.40 W.

Seven bodies are in, or within orbs of, the 11th. The opposition of the Sun to Saturn seems common in the maps of the presidents of the United States, perhaps because of the manner in which they necessarily rise and then fall from power at the end of their term, unlike monarchs, who may retain their purple to the end.

Franklin Roosevelt also has a Sun–Saturn affliction, and Sun square Jupiter and Neptune as well, as also sesquiquadrate Mars.

CASE No. 12.

Franklin D. Roosevelt, born 8 p.m., January 30, 1882, 41.45 N., 74 W. Information from reliable private sources.

To my mind a most instructive map and typical of the "heroic" personality, who steps forward when the battle is at its most critical moment and shoulders burdens when they are most pressing. We must stress what has been said as to the Moon representing the inner and the Sun the outer man. Here the life of action is hard. We know that the native was crippled early in life by a stroke following on sudden immersion in cold water (Sun square Neptune). This paralysis was partly overcome by sheer dogged will. The Moon has the good aspects of ♄ ♆ in ♉, which are in square to the Sun, and the Moon rises as the Sun declines. Mercury, the ruler of the 1st, is weak in the 6th but has a fairly near trine of the elevated Mars, which, with Uranus, is the effective ruler of the horoscope. Uranus, rising, gives personal expression to the Moon sextile Saturn–Neptune–Jupiter formation and these build up a splendid integration, involving cardinal, fixed, and common signs, and angular, succedent, and cadent houses. The Sun and Venus, of course, belong to the same group, but impinge upon it by an abrupt square influence, as difficult physically as it has proved ennobling in its effects on character. Mercury and Mars are, of course, in contact with this group, but may be regarded as forming a second integration.

At this stage we may mention that lack of self-confidence, that sense of personal inadequacy which nowadays receives so much attention under the name of the inferiority complex.

When we consider how helpless and independent we all are in infancy, and how, as we grow up, we have forced upon us on all sides how much wiser, better, and cleverer others are than we, it is not

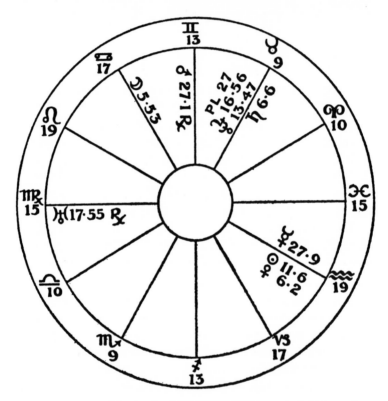

strange that those who possess more sensitivity than resilience of spirit become oppressed with a feeling that they are more or less worthless. In some cases this sensation is perfectly conscious, and the individual in question is then as a rule an openly shy, apologetic type, always acting as if he were depressed by his own futility and aware that others were contemptuous towards him and vexed by his existence. If the feeling is less conscious to the mind of the sufferer there are often attempts to forget its presence and disguise it from others, and these efforts often take the form of arrogance towards inferiors, boasting, and egocentric conversation, all of which is little else than "whistling to keep one's spirits up" and incidentally making oneself a nuisance to others. On the other hand, it is, of course, equally inordinate to be blind to one's abilities and lack of ability; the sane attitude is a correct apprisal of what one is and is not, can and cannot, and an honest desire to make the best of what one has and to take an intelligent interest in life, instead of finding refuge in fantasies and histrionic gestures that are meant to encourage oneself and frighten others, but certainly do not deceive anyone possessing a modicum of understanding. Extreme feelings of inadequacy often occasion violent efforts at self-restoration, just as extreme bodily weakness often leads to the use of powerful and deleterious drugs; thus, in a desperate attempt to restore self-confidence, the mind may be thrown off its balance and the victim conceives some such fantasy as that he is the Almighty. Another possible *dénouement* is religious melancholia and the belief that one is forsaken and damned. Imaginary illness is a frequent remedy; it supplies an excuse for not trying to achieve anything and the victim hopes to experience the flattery of being danced attendance upon.

However, this is not the place to attempt to deal with a very big subject, except to show how it bears upon insanity and lesser forms of mental delusion and disorder. Further, to say something of the astrological characteristics which indicate tendencies of this sort.

I should say that it is in Saturn and Neptune, and

the 12th house, that we see the clearest signs of the inadequacy complex. Probably the majority of people have this ailment in some form, but fortunately only to such an extent as to colour their conduct with certain irrationalities and to diminish their efficiency to a degree that might escape the notice of all but trained observers. A minority are so afflicted as to produce neuroses of a more or less serious character.

A good example of this condition is N.N. 269—"stood in her own light; singularly unlucky, mistrustful, discontented and apprehensive." Here four bodies are in or near the 12th in Gemini and one, the ruler, is opposed to Saturn. Neptune dominates the entire map from the M.C. The Sun, in air, is square Uranus in water above it, and this is a type that we shall see again, for the best recipe to produce mental disorder of this sort is an adverse impact of water on air—the fantasy on the mind. And Pisces affliction directed to Gemini planets seems the commonest form, though Cancer to Libra and Scorpio to Aquarius are also on record. The watery influence spells anxiety, worry, and fear.

Fire is more often panicky, but fire agrees better with air than does water, since they are both positive. However, N.N. 379 (dread of solitude) shows Mars in Sagittarius in direct opposition to an ascendant which is involved in a Mercury–Jupiter–Uranus–Neptune complex. The Moon is in the 12th and Saturn in the 6th—Saturn in any cadent house inclines somewhat to fearfulness. I have other cases of this discomfort when solitary, and in all of them the Sagittarian element is strong.

In the horoscope of one "painfully shy, unable to express himself, and quite inarticulate in company," I find the ruler Mars (Scorpio rises, a sign often socially timid in youth) in the 12th, opposed to the Moon. The

Sun is conjoined with Saturn in the 3rd in Aquarius. The Venus—social contacts—is in Aries, forming a "T" with Uranus and Neptune in opposition. Not a very terribly afflicted horoscope and one may legitimately expect a cure. But the Aquarian conjunction receives the square (though not close) of Mars in water. The two oppositions are significant, for, since this aspect corresponds to the 1st–7th houses, it particularly affects relations with others. I have known somewhat similar configurations in cases where the unfortunate native could not enter society because of an impulse to vomit as soon as he was confronted with strangers!

A case that suggests the inferiority-complex very forcibly to me is N.N. 408—"lad of no moral sense, almost a religious maniac; always attempting tricks that won't come off." Here Sun, Jupiter, and Neptune, in close conjunction, rise in Gemini—a very vain formation—and there is a square to them from Mars in Pisces, as well as a trine to Saturn in Libra. In the child's intense desire to gratify an inner feeling of inferiority he seeks to attract notice and admiration by trying to "work miracles," which, of course, come to nothing; he deludes himself and tries to delude others by repeating that "it didn't go that time but next time it will." In this map the Moon, Pluto, and Mercury are also in Gemini and the mere presence of so many bodies near the ascendant would tend towards vanity. But the man with true self-confidence and self-understanding is not vain. Vanity is merely the weak man's attempt at persuading himself and others that he is what he knows interiorly he is not.

The air-water conflict is strikingly illustrated in the natus of an unfortunate lady born just after midnight, May 7, 1896, at Cairo. At the age of 33½ she was found dead in one of the Hebrides. She was a student of occultism and had constructed a sort of cross in the turf, wherein she laid herself one night and, having a weak heart, succumbed to exposure. The case was reported in the papers.

Once again Mars is in water (Pisces) with the Moon, and both are in square to Neptune and Pluto in Gemini. The Sun is opposed to Saturn and Uranus in Scorpio and Aquarius 4° rising has the opposition of Jupiter, with Venus in square to both.

Without reflecting either on religion or on occultism, it is clear that both may offer to a feeling of inadequacy a relief which may or may not be ultimately beneficial. The test really lies in the reaction produced, whether rational or irrational, useful or useless.

Louis XIV of France probably had an inferiority-complex. Indeed, it is related that as a boy he was neglected and humiliated and his subsequent passion for splendour, court-ritualism, and ceremony, his aggressive wars in search of self-aggrandisement, and his insatiable vanity, all point to an early distortion which spoilt his later life by demanding more and more demonstrations of grandeur to help him to forget the past. His horoscope shows Saturn afflicted in the 3rd house, Jupiter in the 12th, and Neptune near the ascendant in Scorpio. Here, then, Jupiter in water (not Mars, as in the previous cases), supplies one term of the conflict, and Saturn in air the other. But Mars is also in square to Mercury and the Moon and Venus are opposed to Saturn.

An inordinate desire to accumulate a large fortune, without making any particular use of the money, is also a sign, in most cases, of the desire to bolster up an inner feeling of deficiency. But other factors may also operate in such cases and some people make money because they enjoy the excitement of doing so, or almost as a habit. Where there is an inner craving "to die worth so much" there cannot be simply a healthy desire to exercise one's peculiar faculties; there is merely a morbid desire to demonstrate one's superiority over one's fellows in at least one field.

The same urgently felt passion often manifests as sexual gallantry, this being a mode of self-flattery; the successful Don Juan or flirt is always vain and usually has very little to be vain about. Lord Byron, badly brought up and taunted with his club-foot, sought to prove that he was none the less attractive by indulging in innumerable love-affairs, whereas commonsense, if it needed any such proof at all, might have been content with winning the affection of one worthy woman. His nativity is not of established authenticity, and Cancer and Scorpio have both been claimed as his ascending signs, but, in either case, there is a plain air-water conflict in Moon with Uranus in Cancer, square Neptune (bringing in the 12th influence) in Libra. Four bodies in Saturnian signs stressed the sense of the defect.

Byron's reaction to his crippled condition and that of Franklin Roosevelt to his paralysis form an interesting contrast. The former led only to increased neuroticism and an ever deeper entanglement in psychological maladjustment and unhappiness; the latter brought fame and the opportunity to carry out a vast work of public reconstruction. Yet, in his despair, Byron was to some extent saved by his final effort at useful self-expression; and his end in the field, fighting for the freedom of the country he idealized, was his redemption in death, if not in life. We may ascribe this last struggle to the strong Mars–Uranus elements in his natus. The same two planets are strong in Roosevelt's horoscope: they are the planet of *Karma-marga*—the path of redemption by works.

CHAPTER TEN

DIRECTIONAL DELINEATION

PROGNOSTIC astrology as at present understood is based on what may be called concurrent phenomena, such as transits and cognate configurations, and directions. This last is an old word first used in relation to primary directing, in which a body is brought, or directed, from its radical position to another point. Directions are now understood to mean a natural or intellectual (symbolic) movement of a body which is held to signify an event not coincident in time with itself. For example, the passage, by transit, of Mars over my Sun is not a direction, for it will produce a condition within two or three days, at most, of its own occurrence. But if I direct Mars to the conjunction of my Sun, by the secondary system, then the related condition will arise many years after the actual passage of Mars to the Sun. If Mars reached the Sun four days after birth, then, by the usual secondary system, we should say that the directional effect would manifest at four years. All secondary directions are, of course, transits first, and what is a transit at x days of life will become a direction at x years.

It is a golden rule in prognosis that no direction can bring what is not first of all inherent in the nativity. This is the basic principle of directional work and it admits of little, if any, modification. Again, badly afflicted planets produce little good and strong ones little harm, and it is particularly the case that, if a direction is formed between two bodies in aspect at birth, then, though the direction will usually be of a contrary nature to the radical formation, it is likely to be strongly affected by the latter. It is true that bodies will act more strongly by direction if they are radically configured in any manner, than if they have no such radical relation. But if the radical connection be of one nature, the directional will tend to follow it.

For example, if the Sun and Jupiter have no radical relation their progressed aspects may cause nothing very outstanding; if they are in bad aspect, then the progressed trine or sextile will be to some extent vitiated; if they are radically in good aspect their progressions will incline to goodness, even if technically bad.

In judging the strength of directions, i.e. their prominence in the life, consider such points as angularity. A cadent body seldom brings obvious results.

Passing to a consideration of the methods that are or have been in use, we find a wide diversity and are faced with the question as to what system produces the best and most reliable results.

"Primary" directing is based on the axial rotation of the earth, which causes the planets to rise, culminate and set daily, thus forming directional aspects to each other's radical positions and to the horizon and the meridian. When these aspects were reckoned in terms of the ecliptic they were called zodiacal and when in terms of houses they were styled mundane. For example, if 0° Aries rises, then a body might be directed to the point 0° Sagittarius and would then be trine the ascendant "in the zodiac." But if a body is directed to the cusp of the 5th or 9th, it is then in "mundane" trine to the ascendant, being four houses distant from it. These classes were distinguished by the abbreviations, *dz.* = direction in the zodiac and *mundo* = in the world, or mundanely. They were also divided into direct and converse, according to the sense of the motion by which they were formed.

This system was mathematical and made a heavy demand on the student's time and patience, and even on his arithmetical abilities. An enthusiast might calculate his *own* primaries, but few were willing to do more! Moreover, the results were more imposing to the eye and ear than to the critical faculty. Long lists of directions were tabulated, but they were more formidable in appearance than in anything that they produced in the life.

It may be said that the "primary" system flourished during the middle ages and almost up to our own times. When, in the '90's, astrology began to interest more than a small body of people and the professional astrologer had to deal with many clients, it became necessary to seek something better than the primaries, which were already ceasing to be an integral and necessary part of astrology at the commencement of this century.

"Sepharial" (Walter Gornold) wrote on the primary system, but he is generally held to have introduced the "progressed horoscope" which Alan Leo popularized. This, in a measure, combined the "primary" and "secondary" systems—terms, by the way, which might well be discarded.

"Secondary" or Arabian directions are familiar to the student as the day-for-a-year system in which the natural movements of the planets are translated directionally at the rate of 24 hours = a year.

DIRECTIONAL DELINEATION

The progressed horoscope is obtained by adding or subtracting, as the case may be, the time of birth to or from the successive sidereal times on each noon after birth. Thus there is a progression not only of the planets but of the angles, which, by their movement through the zodiac, form aspects which are of great importance with radical bodies.

This device is probably the method in widest use at the present day.

It has been supplemented by various symbolical measures first introduced by Mr. W. Frankland and by the present writer in the years 1928–1929, but whether we use these, in addition to the progressed horoscope or instead of it, we must pay due attention to transits, including in that word eclipses and lunations.

These are of great importance and, since we are in a work of this kind chiefly concerned with the means of obtaining a general conspectus of the life, its main lines of unfoldment, mental and circumstantial, we must emphasize that the passage of the major planets through the houses are influences not lightly to be estimated in regard to their significance. These *domal* transits, sometimes called ingresses, appear to me to merit careful attention, and none the less because we are here involved in no technical difficulties, such as occur in more complicated methods. We have only to watch the bodies as they move in the skies and are set down in the ephemeris.

Their special natal peculiarities must always be borne in mind and, in particular, their relation to the house they are passing through. For example, if Jupiter is natally in affliction with the ruler of the 10th, his transit through that house will do no good, or but little. If he is no aspect at all with the ruler, his action will be but moderate. If he is in strong good aspect, then his benefits will be notable, especially if he is angular and well configured at birth. If he is natally weak, then, being Jupiter, he may be well-intentioned, but, being weak, he is but a well-intentioned beggar who can bestow little assistance, wherever he goes.

But normally Jupiter brings the affairs of the houses through which he passes to the fore and imports into them something of his own nature and the matters of the houses he rules; he promotes what he touches.

Saturn can be helpful but he introduces a serious and even a perditive note and often brings heavy responsibilities.

Uranus and Neptune move, of course, very slowly and cover long periods, operating according to their natures when in aspect to radical positions. They do not always act when their transits are exact and perhaps that has led students to think these unimportant; this is not my own belief. I think that the transits—especially the conjunctions and oppositions—of these two are as important as powerful directions. But they must be watched in perspective.

Also I have noticed that they sometimes produce their maximum effect, so far as distinct events go, at a time exactly between two successive transits to the same points, as they go direct and retrograde. For example, I had Neptune T.[1] opposite the Sun rad. on February 22nd, 1921, and on June 18. The intervening period = 116 days, and if we add half of this to the former date we get April 21st. My father died on April 25th. Now, had I looked for results from these

[1] My abbreviation to denote transitual action.

130

transits that were close in time, I might have concluded that there were none; but a knowledge of this little law shows how important, in fact, a transit can be.

Indeed, it is the hope, if but a pious one, of many astrologers that a complete system based only on transits may be discovered, so great are the advantages of work based on these phenomena when contrasted with the directional systems, all of which are to a greater or less extent symbolical, or based on correspondences. Now, no correspondence can be as clear as direct action, such as transits exhibit.

At present it may seem that this hope is altogether impossible because the motions of the Sun, Moon, and minor planets are so quick that their transits are too frequently repeated to have much significance, whilst the transits of the majors are too uncommon to cover all the changes of life. Whether this objection is sound I will not say. So far as personal experience goes I believe that three-quarters, at least, of the events of my not uneventful life could be adequately accounted for by transits, properly understood.

Lunations and eclipses are, of course, transits when considered in relation to the individual horoscope; They are, in fact, double impacts, the two bodies forming a conjunction on a sensitive place. The ordinary lunation usually produces, if it touches such a spot, a very sensible but not severe result, lasting a few days, before and after exactitude. Eclipses, however, which are lunations wherein the lights form a direct, or nearly direct, line with the centre of the earth, are much stronger, even when not visible at the place of birth or residence, and their effects continue, off and on, for protracted periods, perhaps for six months or a year.

Transits of all sorts may be studied in respect of progressed bodies but are not usually regarded as being as important as transits to radical points.

After a consideration of transits of all kinds attention may be directed to that extremely important class of direction, comprising the aspects formed by the progressed ascendant and midheaven.

It is almost incredible, but it is nevertheless true, that some astrologers are so infatuated as to disregard these formations, which, by the testimony of every student of note since the days of Ptolemy, as well as the experience of thousands of the rank and file, are known to be amongst the most potent of all stellar indices, producing, almost if not quite invariably, events of an epochal character. The aspects of the progressed Sun can alone vie with this class in respect of importance and, somewhat lower in the scale perhaps, come aspects formed by progressed bodies to the radical angles. Of directions proper these are the true primaries and a careful study of them will reveal the main chapters of the life under consideration. Parallels should not be overlooked because they involve a trifle more trouble than ecliptical directions. One important period of my life began under asc. par. Jupiter and another under Sun par. Uranus.

Another rare, but important type of direction occurs when a major (slow-moving) body[1] completes an aspect already within orbs at birth. This lasts for a long period or, if of an acute kind, produces an important event. I was born under Sun trine Uranus, 35' apart; this became exact, by the local motion of Uranus to the radical Sun, at the age of 23 and coincided with my

---

[1] A minor planet may, of course, also be slow of motion but will not, even then, equal a major in strength.

coming to the light of astrology, Sun trine Jupiter being also operative.

Planets becoming stationary are the most important, being then extremely potent. To continue personal instances, Mercury became stationary when *Astrology* was started and Saturn stationary was my chief personal reminder of the Great Depression of 1930–33.

The above constitute, in my experience, the epoch-making, or epoch-indicating, classes of phenomena, so far as natural indices go.

Interplanetary directions were not used by the old primarists, but this absurd rule need not be regarded in day-for-a-year directing and was doubtless due to the fact that, if such directions had been admitted, the student would have been overwhelmed with the number of influences, zodiacal and mundane, that he would have found before him. Day-for-a-year interplanetaries are not, usually, of first-class importance, but they are valid enough and make "make or mar" the fortune of six months or so, influencing and to some extent colouring the minor indices operative during the period of their predominance.

Lunar secondaries are useful chronocrators, indicating when more potent influences will precipitate. In themselves they do not act for longer than a month or so, always excepting, I think, the conjunctions and oppositions, which, in *all* astrology, are much the most potent contacts. A lunar conjunction or opposition can, I should say, act for several months, especially if other similar influences are in operation.

Mention must be made of what are called pre-natal secondaries, or, by some, converse secondaries, in which the count is made backwards instead of forward from the time of birth, the same day-to-a-year measure being employed and there being no difference in the method of interpretation. These converse secondaries are by some regarded as equal in strength to the direct, whilst there are not lacking those who consign the whole "secondary" system to limbo or declare that it is of use so long as it is considered to be what it is called, i.e. secondary to more potent influences. There is, in fact, no species of prognostic operation which has not been condemned as worthless by someone, or, at least, such is my impression after almost a quarter of a century of astrological activity. Nor is the *odium theologicum* always an easy first in comparison with the *odium astrologicum.*

We pass now to the symbolic methods already mentioned. These were introduced because the progressed horoscope, shorn of the support of the primaries that are now obsolescent and were never worth a great deal, seemed inadequate.

Time has allowed the many students who have tried the symbolic measures to sift them, numerous as they are. I have found the most reliable to be the $2\frac{1}{2}° =$ a year as a quick measure, $1° =$ a year as a medium measure, and $\frac{1}{4}°$ and $\frac{1}{8}° =$ a year as slow measures which occur comparatively rarely. All these can be employed as supplements to the transits and secondaries and angular progressions; and I should certainly be sorry to lose them as, in my own case, I have never found them to fail to work, and I have never yet, in very numerous cases, found that an event was recorded to which there was not an appropriate coincident symbolic direction. Their simplicity is, of course, a great recommendation, though obviously a worthless one, were they not also reliable in practice.

My own experience is that they tend to work at the

time of exactitude or shortly afterwards, but that their *full* operation is often delayed for as long as three months, depending, of course, like other major influences, on the excitatory activity of lesser influences.

If I abandoned all others I would at least retain the $1° =$ a year measure.

Of this the older "radix" measure is a near relation. In this the progression is 59′ 8″ to the year, in place of one degree, i.e. the mean solar increment.

For information concerning the measures and methods introduced by Mr. Frankland the reader is referred to his books. In my own work on the subject numerous symbolic measures are explained and examples are adduced to show their efficacy. It is, however, not intended that in practice all these increments should be employed, but that they should be tested and that each student should adopt those that he finds most effective. The above four progressions are my own selection and, since two of them are very slow, they do not overburden one's directional sheet, especially as personally I never use the minor aspects in symbolic directing. The conjunction, opposition, square, trine, and sextile appear to be all that are required and, for that matter, they are all that would be normally used in any directing that had as its aim the discovery of the chief movements in the life, adding only the parallel of declination.

Other directional systems exist, some known only to individuals and some only to small groups, but the above is a synopsis of general practice at the present moment. In certain circles there is a strong dislike of the symbolic methods and the question of the place that these will occupy after another twenty-five years or so can only be a matter of conjecture.

The ideal directional system would provide an event, or at least some appropriate unfoldment, for each direction, and a direction for each event, each appropriate to each and also synchronous within a reasonable limit. Nay, some would say that almost the minute of an event should be previsible, as well as its nature and intensity. Whether we shall ever reach this stage and whether life would be better if we did, one may be permitted to doubt. The system outlined here does not tie man down to predestination, but it will give meaning and interest to life and be of practical value also, since to be forewarned is to be forearmed.

*   *   *   *   *

The question has often been asked—and will often be asked again, especially in reference to prognosis— what is the *use* of astrology? I would reply that man is, at least in his more human moments, a reasoning creature to whom the idea that life is essentially unreasonable and chaotic must always appear distressing. It is astrology, the "grand old science," as our forerunners called it, that can demonstrate how very far from chaotic life is, even in its apparently widest aberrations from reason, and prognostic astrology shows in what orderly ways our lives unfold their meanings. This, in my experience, greatly tends to satisfy the soul and soothe its moments of tribulations. Indeed, if I may speak personally, after almost a quarter-of-a-century of astrological study, astrology not only assists us to direct our lives wisely when it is in our power to do so, but it teaches us also to endure bravely whatever may be beyond our present powers to alter or control.

BOOKS ON ASTROLOGY
by CHARLES E. O. CARTER

●

AN ENCYCLOPAEDIA OF
PSYCHOLOGICAL ASTROLOGY
With observations on the astrological characteristics of about fifty diseases and an introductory essay on the zodiacal signs. Third edition revised and enlarged.

SYMBOLIC DIRECTIONS IN
MODERN ASTROLOGY
Symbolic Directing occupies but a fraction of the time required for the measures in common use.

THE ZODIAC AND THE SOUL
A treatise on the most profound aspects of astrology ; it reveals in clear language the essential Ideas that arc portrayed in the symbols of Astrology.

THE ASTROLOGICAL ASPECTS
One of the most helpful books that have appeared in recent years, containing an entirely original study of the values of the various astrological aspects, based on a large collection of actual cases.

SOME PRINCIPLES OF HOROSCOPIC
DELINEATION
Containing Ten Chapters on the Scope of the Nativity : —The Aspects—Mundane position—Sign position—Planetary Psychology—Infant Mortality and Longevity—Suicide and Insanity—The Violent Criminal—Outstanding Ability and Failure.

Better books make better astrologers.
Here are some of our other titles:

___

AstroAmerica's Daily Ephemeris, 2010-2020
AstroAmerica's Daily Ephemeris, 2000-2020
  - *all for Midnight. Compiled & formatted by David R. Roell*

Al Biruni
The Book of Instructions in the Elements of the Art of
  Astrology, *1029 AD, translated by R. Ramsay Wright*

Derek Appleby
Horary Astrology: The Art of Astrological Divination

E. H. Bailey
The Prenatal Epoch

C.E.O. Carter
An Encyclopaedia of Psychological Astrology
The Principles of Astrology, *Intermediate no. 1*
Some Principles of Horoscopic Delineation, *Intermediate no. 2*

Charubel & Sepharial
Degrees of the Zodiac Symbolized, *1898*

H.L. Cornell, M.D.
Encyclopaedia of Medical Astrology
  958 pages, hardcover, the ultimate astro-medical reference

Nicholas Culpeper
Astrological Judgement of Diseases from the Decumbiture of
  the Sick, *1655, and,* **Urinalia**, *1658*

Dorotheus of Sidon
Carmen Astrologicum, *c. 50 AD, translated by David Pingree*

Nicholas deVore
Encyclopedia of Astrology

Firmicus Maternus
Ancient Astrology Theory & Practice: Matheseos Libri VIII,
c. 350 AD, translated by Jean Rhys Bram

William Lilly
Christian Astrology, books 1 & 2, *1647*
   The Introduction to Astrology, Resolution of all manner of questions.
Christian Astrology, book 3, *1647*
   Easie and plaine method teaching how to judge upon nativities.

Alan Leo
The Progressed Horoscope, *1905*

Claudius Ptolemy
Tetrabiblos, *c. 140 AD, translated by J.M. Ashmand*
   The great book, in the classic translation.

Vivian Robson
Astrology and Sex
Electional Astrology
Fixed Stars & Constellations in Astrology

Richard Saunders
The Astrological Judgement and Practice of Physick, *1677*
   By the Richard who inspired Ben Franklin's famous Almanac.

Sepharial
Primary Directions, a definitive study
   A complete, detailed guide.

Sepharial On Money. *For the first time in one volume, complete texts:*
   • **Law of Values**
   • **Silver Key**
   • **Arcana, or Stock and Share Key** — *first time in print!*

James Wilson, Esq.
Dictionary of Astrology
   From 1820. Quirky, opinionated, a fascinating read.

H.S. Green, Raphael & C.E.O. Carter
Mundane Astrology: *3 Books, complete in one volume.*
   A comprehensive guide to political astrology

If not available from your local bookseller, order directly from:
The Astrology Center of America
207 Victory Lane
Bel Air, MD 21014

on the web at:
http://www.astroamerica.com

CPSIA information can be obtained at www.ICGtesting.com
Printed in the USA
BVOW05s2033140514

353333BV00001B/33/P

9 781933 303277